T0323591

Cambridge Elements ≡

Elements in Public and Nonprofit Administration
edited by
Andrew Whitford
University of Georgia
Robert Christensen
Brigham Young University

PUBLIC SERVICE EXPLAINED

The Role of Citizens in Value Creation

Greta Nasi
Bocconi University

Stephen P. Osborne
The University of Edinburgh

Maria Cucciniello
Bocconi University

Tie Cui
The University of Edinburgh

CAMBRIDGE
UNIVERSITY PRESS

Shaftesbury Road, Cambridge CB2 8EA, United Kingdom

One Liberty Plaza, 20th Floor, New York, NY 10006, USA

477 Williamstown Road, Port Melbourne, VIC 3207, Australia

314–321, 3rd Floor, Plot 3, Splendor Forum, Jasola District Centre, New Delhi – 110025, India

103 Penang Road, #05–06/07, Visioncrest Commercial, Singapore 238467

Cambridge University Press is part of Cambridge University Press & Assessment, a department of the University of Cambridge.

We share the University's mission to contribute to society through the pursuit of education, learning and research at the highest international levels of excellence.

www.cambridge.org
Information on this title: www.cambridge.org/9781009532914

DOI: 10.1017/9781009373586

First published 2024

A catalogue record for this publication is available from the British Library

ISBN 978-1-009-53291-4 Hardback
ISBN 978-1-009-37359-3 Paperback
ISSN 2515-4303 (online)
ISSN 2515-429X (print)

Cambridge University Press & Assessment has no responsibility for the persistence or accuracy of URLs for external or third-party internet websites referred to in this publication and does not guarantee that any content on such websites is, or will remain, accurate or appropriate.

Public Service Explained

The Role of Citizens in Value Creation

Elements in Public and Nonprofit Administration

DOI: 10.1017/9781009373586
First published online: December 2024

Greta Nasi
Bocconi University

Stephen P. Osborne
The University of Edinburgh

Maria Cucciniello
Bocconi University

Tie Cui
The University of Edinburgh

Author for correspondence: Greta Nasi, greta.nasi@unibocconi.it

Abstract: This Cambridge Element aims to advance theory by investigating the nature of participation in public service delivery. It situates itself under the theory of Public Service Logic to advocate for a strategic orientation to participation as an element of value creation in public services. It introduces the concept of participation and discusses the motives, incentives, and tools to engage citizens in public service delivery processes. Then, it frames citizens' participation under the approach public service ecosystem to capture the dynamic relationships among citizens, other actors, processes, and structures that may contribute to determining value in public service delivery. It presents the dynamics of value creation and destruction in public service. The Element concludes with implications for research and practice. This title is also available as Open Access on Cambridge Core.

Keywords: Public Service Logic, participation, public service ecosystem, value creation, citizens

ISBNs: 9781009532914 (HB), 9781009373593 (PB), 9781009373586 (OC)
ISSNs: 2515-4303 (online), 2515-429X (print)

Contents

Introduction

The relationship between public service delivery and citizen participation is complex and dynamic. The most compelling narratives on public service reforms of recent times – New Public Administration (NPA), New Public Management (NPM), Public Value (PV), New Public Service (NPS), and New Public Governance (NPG) – have investigated how citizen and user participation has been framed. However, despite the proposed advantages and the range of manners of participation across these narratives, they found that despite a plethora of rhetoric, participation has continued to be a chimaera, often relegated to the periphery of public service production (Osborne et al. 2022).

This Element offers an alternative theoretical narrative, grounded in Public Service Logic (PSL) theory that emphasizes participation not as an add-on or normative element of public service delivery but as a core component. Citizens and users play a central role in value creation for themselves and society. Public Service Logic refers to the underlying principles, values, and objectives that guide the design and delivery of public services. It is embedded in the idea that public services should be responsive, effective, equitable, as well as accountable to the needs of citizens and society. On the other hand, participation refers to the involvement of citizens, stakeholders, and communities in the design and delivery of public services.

Public service organizations (PSOs) often fail to foster participation, resulting in inward-looking goal-setting and decision-making processes (Rose et al. 2018). However, participation in public services can provide PSOs with vital feedback on their jobs by alerting them about changes in service priorities, the clientele they serve, or the need to reallocate scarce resources (An and Meier 2022). Moreover, if value creation is a goal of PSO, reconciling what citizens expect from a service and how they perceive its significance is essential for service delivery (Petrovsky et al. 2017). Under PSL, citizens co-create value when a public service is used, and their satisfaction and service value depend upon the service experience (Osborne, Nasi, and Powell 2021). This suggests that incorporating their knowledge into creating, planning, and designing public services enables PSOs to meet better their expectations and needs (Bovaird and Loeffler 2012).

The existing literature acknowledges that citizens are not passive receivers of public services. Instead, they are valuable participants in delivering public services (Osborne and Brown 2011a). However, studying the motives of citizen participation in public services is still embryonic. (Osborne 2020).

Citizens have specific resources (such as time, expertise, and local knowledge) that can be used in response to contemporary public sector problems.

This has resulted in a variety of policy domains in which citizens participate in public service delivery, such as public transport (Gebauer et al. 2010), health, and social care (Pestoff 2012a), and education (Jakobsen 2013; Ostrom 1996). Given the increasing importance of service delivery, recent studies explore how citizens can be motivated, why they would step in and co-produce critical public services, resulting in value co-creation for their own lives (e.g., Alford 2002; Andersen et al. 2017; Jakobsens and Andersen 2013; Moseley et al. 2018; Voorberg et al. 2018).

Only a few scholarly papers examine the outside-in perspective, in which participation informs service design and delivery, allowing for value co-creation (Hardyman et al. 2019; Trischler et al. 2019). Consequently, we need a greater understanding of the motivational factors that encourage citizens to engage in co-production and value creation.

This Cambridge Element aims to advance theory by investigating the nature of participation in public service delivery. It situates it under the theory of PSL to advocate for a strategic orientation to participation as an element of value creation in public services. Our work builds on the long-term research initiatives of the authors.

This Element first reviews the concept of participation in public services in the existing public administration and management (PAM) literature, and then situates it within PSL (Section 1). The following section (Section 2) introduces the concept of participation, discussing the motives, incentives, and tools to engage citizens in public service delivery processes. Then, Section 3 frames citizens' participation under the approach public service ecosystem (PSE) to capture the dynamic relationships among citizens, other actors, processes, and structures that may contribute to determining value in public service delivery. Section 4 presents the dynamics of value creation and destruction in public service. The final section articulates the volume's contribution and suggests a future research plan. We hope to inspire scholars to advance further the intrinsic value of participation in public service processes and ecosystems.

1 Citizen Engagement and Trajectories of Public Service Reform

Since the 1960s, five influential narratives of reform with PAM have shaped the debate on participation. These have evolved chronologically but have often overlapped in time and been influenced by one another. Each of them has articulated a narrative of participation – though its definition and rationale have changed over time, as the analysis here notes. This section explores why these discourses saw public participation in service delivery as necessary (despite criticisms in the case of the NPM) and how they sought to enact it.

For example, NPA and NPS embedded a normative approach to participation as a 'good thing', addressing the democratic deficit in society and as a counterbalance to the power of social elites and public service officials (LaPorte 1971). In contrast, NPM has been criticized, for its disregard for citizen and service user participation, except in the narrow economic sense of the self-interested consumer and the promotion of managerialism and consumerism. New Public Governance began as an entirely descriptive approach to 'actually existing' public services and the role of citizens in their co-production (Osborne 2010) and thence developed into a normative theory of Collaborative Governance that argued for participation as a route to transparent and responsive public services (Sorensen and Torfing 2018). Finally, PV has articulated a discourse of participation that situated this element as part of networked attempts to enhance the effectiveness of public services through such prescribed mechanisms as consultation processes and formal hearings (Horner and Hutton 2011). Table 1 portrays the key dimensions of these five reform narratives, and the subsequent analysis discusses them in more detail with reference to their stance on participation.

1.1 New Public Administration (NPA)

In reaction to the perceived failings of traditional Public Administration (PA), early NPA scholars argued for restoring democratic values by placing citizens at the centre of public service decision-making (White 1971). This aim was to be facilitated predominantly by structural changes, such as decentralization and delayering, and required the active involvement of civic-minded and educated citizens (Frederickson 1980).

Whilst the participation narrative is still broadly situated in the public sector context, it has been impacted by the subsequent hegemonic influence of the NPM (e.g., Vigoda and Golembiewski 2001). With social equity as its defining feature, NPA argued against the hegemony of the private sector norms associated with NPM. The NPA narrative has been criticized for having had only limited impact upon actual public service reform (Denhardt and Denhardt 2015). There is also a lack of empirical evidence explaining how the structural changes proposed by NPA can enable greater participation or social inclusion. Finally, NPA has been criticized for facilitating the participation of articulate citizens and elites, rather than the marginalized groups intended (Ingraham and Rosenbloom 1989).

1.2 The New Public Management (NPM)

From the 1980s onwards, NPM has developed as the pre-eminent narrative of public service reform. It emerged from critiques of PA strongly linked to

Table 1 Participation within the five narratives (adapted from Osborne and Strokosch 2022).

Elements of participations			Theories		
	NPA	NPM	PV	NPS	NPG
Rationale	Dissemination of power, accountability, and legitimacy	Enhancing services and cost reduction	Creation of public value and societal learning	Democratic revitalization and legitimacy	Negotiation of interests and service enhancement
Locus	Political discourse	Service assessment	Indirect engagement through representative democracy	Deliberation during entire service cycle	Inter-organizational collaboration and service provision
Mechanisms	Decentralization and advocacy	Implementation of market mechanisms	Political deliberation and networks formation	Fostering active citizenship through deliberation	Collaboration networks and co-production

a political agenda that centred on the privatization and marketization of public service provision to 'roll back the state' (Hood et al. 1988). New Public Management has been widely criticized for disregarding citizen participation because of its managerialism (Christensen and Laegreid 2011) and its consumerism (Powell et al. 2010). These strands reconstituted citizens as self-interested and passive consumers. New Public Management sought to empower citizens by exercising individual preferences in the markets/quasi-markets for public services, but not by active participation in the service delivery process. This discourse privileged public managers as 'experts', a distinction reinforcing existing power asymmetries between such managers and citizens based on education and expertise. It has also been subject to critique for the atomization of citizens and the undermining of their collective power (Millward 2005).

The late 1980s witnessed a range of reforms that tried to match the citizenship focus of NPA with the consumerist focus of the NPM through, for example, consumer councils (Stewart and Clarke 1987). However, participation here has typically been framed as an opportunity to reduce costs and increase efficiency rather than to enhance service effectiveness or democracy (Lowndes et al. 2001).

1.3 Public Value (PV)

Public Value emerged as a challenge to NPM in the 1990s and expressed a more collaborative approach with the intent of creating 'public value'. It originated with the seminal work of Moore (1995) who developed a normative model of strategic development for public managers that emphasized the pursuit of PV. Public Value has subsequently developed into a broad narrative with nuances within it – as a theoretical framework that emphasizes public service improvement (Benington 2011), a normative narrative (Alford and O'Flynn 2009), and/ or a governance framework (Bryson et al. 2014).

Despite these variations, participation is a central construct of the PV narrative and is typically offered as a means of addressing the limits of representative democracy (Yang 2016). There is a strong focus in PV on political interaction through networks of deliberation between elected/appointed government officials and civil society with the purpose of facilitating negotiation, cooperation, and decision-making among diverse groups (O'Flynn 2007). Participation is operationalized predominantly through formal (e.g., public hearings) and informal (e.g., lobbying) networks.

Creating PV is reliant on citizens' participation in the decision-making stage to understand their needs, concerns and aspirations. Moreover, recognizing that today's complex societal challenges cannot be effectively addressed by individual (public) organizations alone, the creation of PV during the service-delivery stage equally relies on cooperative efforts involving multiple actors, including the participation of citizens mainly through third sectors, community organizations and civil society. In this regard, PV narrative suits the emergence of networked/ collaborative governance (Stoker 2006). The efforts to integrate discourses on collaborative governance and PV narrative have therefore been gaining attention in recent years (Bryson et al. 2014). Relevant research has sought to provide a normative approach to articulate the importance of collaborative arrangements in creating and safeguarding PV. However, criticisms are raised related to the challenges in coordinating actions, addressing power asymmetries, and ensuring accountability. When poorly organized, collaborative governance can result in PV failure (Williams et al. 2016).

A core criticism of PV is its having been developed as a polemic against NPM, but with limited evidence of its own efficacy (Williams and Shearer 2011). Further, whilst citizens are described as active, participative, and responsible, PV also defines public managers as 'creative entrepreneurs' who translate policy into proposals about what is valuable (Moore and Benington 2011) and who, crucially, control the extent of participation, thereby reinforcing traditional power relations (Dahl and Soss 2014). Finally, like NPA, PV has also been reproached for the disproportionate inclusion of organized and articulate elites at the expense of marginal and informal groupings (Williams and Shearer 2011).

1.4 New Public Service (NPS)

New Public Service emerged from the US in the early 2000s (Denhardt and Denhardt 2000). It developed from a critique of NPM and a desire to replace it with an open and accessible system of governance, within which the citizen becomes central to decision-making throughout the public service delivery cycle. New Public Service is underpinned by three theoretical perspectives: democratic citizenship, which demands greater citizen engagement and a shared vision of 'public interest'; models of community and civil society, where the government plays a key role in the renewal of civil society; and 'organizational humanism' with a focus on the needs and preferences of citizens, rather than bureaucratic control or objective performance measurements (deLeon and Denhardt 2000). New Public Service proposes a 'virtuous circle', where participation is defined as of intrinsic value to citizens and leads to their taking greater civic responsibility – which, in turn, catalyses further participation in public service delivery (Denhardt and Denhardt 2015). Structural changes are paramount to the NPS agenda, with the role of government 'to serve rather than steer'. It acts as the negotiator, enabler, and facilitator of collaborative relationships, and public managers play a key role as 'transformative leaders' (Jun and Bryer 2017).

Although NPS takes a strong normative stance, its arguments for participation have not been substantiated by empirical research. Its focus on structural changes, for example, suggests an oversimplification of participation in practice, by overlooking the need to carefully organize and facilitate the *processes* of participation (Fischer 2006) or to account for the disproportionate influence of social elites. Furthermore, the NPS argument that participation should be institutionalized is hard to implement because it assumes that all citizens have a latent desire for participation that can be awakened. Yet, there is a scarcity of evidence to validate this argument (Brugue and Gallego 2003).

1.5 New Public Governance (NPG)

Finally, NPG was first articulated by Osborne (2010) to describe the impact that approaches to network governance and collaboration within 'actually existing' public service delivery have upon PAM. Consequently, NPG built on organizational sociology and network theory to suggest that public management is enacted by networks of actors from the for-profit, public and third sector. Within this narrative, participation was framed in two ways. First, 'co-production' was integrated and repositioned within this narrative. Re-conceptualized as co-producers (rather than as consumers, as in the NPM), citizens were here described as working in a horizontal, interactive and co-operative relationship with government (Pestoff 2012b). The potential advantages of co-production were discussed widely in the NPG literature, including its potential to increase democracy and tackle challenging social issues (Bovaird 2007).

There has been extensive debate surrounding the varieties of co-production in public services. Researchers have suggested different taxonomies based on 'who', 'when', 'what outcomes' of co-production (Nabatchi et al. 2017). More research has further explored the context in which and the reasons for which co-production should take place (Steiner et al. 2022). Additionally, recent years have witnessed a growing discourse about the relationship between service co-production and value co-creation (Voorberg et al. 2015).

Second, a new generation of research has repositioned the NPG as a normative framework of 'collaborative governance'. This work has examined the democratic capacity of various actors to work in co-operative relationships to achieve societal consensus. It has been argued to both increase democracy and reduce the cost of public services (Sorensen and Torfing 2018).

Whilst it has been welcomed for involving a plurality of actors, the inclusiveness of NPG has been questioned. Critics have argued that, in practice, network membership was exclusive to those with the necessary organizational infrastructure, expertise, knowledge, and skills and who could hence manipulate the system for their own gains (Van Tatenhove et al. 2010). In practice, such networks enhanced inter-organizational engagement across PSOs but did not produce greater participation of citizens/communities (Greenaway et al. 2007).

Research on the 'dark side' of co-production has also become more prominent recently (Williams et al. 2016). It has been criticized for its tendency to benefit disproportionately the well-off sections of society and for its confinement to public services that have already been designed by public managers and for the control over the provision of opportunities for participation that it cedes to public managers (Thomsen 2017). Such criticism raises important questions concerning the extent to which co-production, and the NPG, can lead to genuine citizen participation or whether it is a 'de facto' management tool to retain and strengthen existing managerial and/or elite power (Alford 2009).

1.6 Participation and Public Services: An Alternative Approach

Participation in public service delivery has thus been a recurrent element in the major public service reform narratives since the 1960s. However, the motivations behind, processes of, and intended outcomes have varied across the five narratives studied here. These have included expressive and instrumental rationales for participation, both an end in its own right and/or a means to achieve more effective public services (e.g., Sorensen and Torfing 2018). Our analysis suggests that citizen participation has remained on the periphery of decision-making structures. The normative stance of some of the narratives is one barrier to its achievement, alongside the hegemony of a linear model of public service delivery, a preoccupation with structural rather than processual change, and a failure to address the power imbalances endemic to public services. Crucially, four of the narratives discussed here identified participation as something to be 'added into' traditional public service delivery, whilst PV identified it as an effective public service delivery outcome. In reality, though, only limited achievements in user participation in public service delivery have been demonstrated over the last fifty years (Roberts 2004). Co-production, for example, has been positioned in several of these reform narratives as a significant route to the achievement of participation in public service delivery (Nabatchi et al. 2017). However, iterative studies have identified that co-production, in isolation, is itself subject to the systemic problems of power asymmetry and elite capture already identified (Flemig and Osborne 2019).

To counter these limitations, we argue for an approach to public service reform that builds on and integrates the *extrinsic* forms of participation, but which also draws upon the unique insights of service management and marketing (SM&M) theory to understand the *intrinsic* modes of participation which characterize services – including public services. This approach has become known latterly as PSL and is an evolving one in the PAM literature (e.g., Dudau et al. 2019; Hodgkinson et al. 2017; Osborne 2021). It is also one that arguably offers a public service reform framework that has participation at its centre rather than periphery.

The PSL approach to participation in public service delivery has seven distinct features. First, it appreciates that public services are a concrete expression of extant societal values and that participation needs to be understood within this values-based framework (Flinders et al. 2016). Such societal values will shape the nature and impact of participation in public service delivery. Public managers cannot shape such societal values but they do need to understand and respond to them, as the PV discourse has appreciated. Public Service Logic situates such values within the PSE that is the context for citizen participation in public service delivery (Osborne et al. 2022; Strokosch and Osborne 2020).

Second, PSL argues that the delivery of public services is not a linear production process of the turning of inputs into outputs, nor is it the sole responsibility of public managers. Rather it is a complex and interactive space where both citizens and public service users interact with societal values and norms, PSOs, the local community, and service delivery processes. Responsive public service delivery is thus not a matter of internal efficacy alone or dependent on the single-handed transformative capacity of public managers as often articulated in the reform narratives, as Pollitt and Boukaert (2017) have noted. Rather it is rather a dynamic process of interaction, negotiation and co-operation between multiple actors, including citizens, and other resources at various levels of the system (Skålén et al. 2018). Citizen participation, therefore, needs to be understood within these complex and dynamic PSEs, instead of focusing predominantly upon the structural features of public service delivery and reform (Leite and Hodgkinson 2021).

Third, recent innovations in SM&M theory have moved to identify participation as a core determinant of the value that a user derives from a service: the experience of participation creates expressive value for the service user and instrumental value concerning their needs (Vargo and Lusch 2008). Public Service Logic theory explores the nature of such value and its creation and its implications for the role of citizens in public service delivery (Hardyman et al. 2019; Osborne et al. 2021).

Fourth, user participation is an intrinsic element of producing public services 'as services' (Osborne 2021). It is not something to be 'added into' service delivery but rather an element of the process that has to be governed and worked with by service providers – it cannot be avoided (Grönroos and Voima 2013). Intrinsic participation processes will thus shape the nature of the public service by bringing the user's expectations, experiences and needs into the service delivery process. Public services will also shape the public service user's whole-life experience by how the experience of receiving a service affects their immediate personal well-being and their future expectations of their capacity in society. Positioning public service users and their 'lived experience' of service as a defining dimension of its delivery reframes their role from passive consumer who is acted upon, to active service producer and value creator. In contrast to the previous narratives, PSL thus understands public service users as actors who are integral to the realization of their own needs. The core task of public management is to facilitate and support this 'actually existing' participation, rather than to ignore or undermine it.

Fifth, participation can also be extrinsic to public service delivery, as articulated within the PAM discourse. In this case, it can be consciously added into public service delivery through co-design and co-production (Trischler and Westman-Trischler 2022). However, the extrinsic processes of participation endorsed by the previous narratives have, to date, been insufficiently persuasive in reorientating away from NPM's unprecedented emphasis on internal organizational efficacy at the expense of collectively held PVs (Nabatchi 2018). By emphasizing the complexity rather than the linearity of the public service production process and the intrinsic processes of participation, PSL supports a deeper reorientation towards the values-based framework centred on the user and societal needs it reflects.

Combining points four and five, it is helpful to make a further clarification. From a PSL perspective, user participation is viewed as an intrinsic element in public service delivery, while co-production, as one type of participation, is extrinsic and thus, optional (Trischler and Charles 2019). For some services like health care that rely on professions and expertise, it is difficult for users to co-produce services. While their role as service users is still inalienable, and their cooperation matters the service outcome. In fact, no matter how a public service is produced and prepared, whether through a co-production format or not, it should be used by users to create value. In this regard, again, user participation is indispensable. However, we do recognize that in some cases, like prison, service use can be coercive and compulsory. Sixth, participation has import for multiple actors in the PSE, not only the identified service user. Citizens who are not users of a public service can also accrue value, perhaps through a role as a volunteer or carer in a public service, but it can also be through the way that participation in public service delivery enables societal value, such as social inclusion or environmental enhancement (Musso et al. 2019). Needless to say, individual and societal values are not always congruent and can sometimes conflict (Benington 2011). Further, even individuals who are not citizens can accrue value through participation in public service delivery – such as tourists (Soszyński et al. 2018) or asylum seekers (Strokosch and Osborne 2016).

Seventh, participation is not a zero sum game for public services. It is as possible to destroy individual and societal value through participation as to create it (Cui and Osborne 2023a). The service user can destroy value when they refuse to participate according to procedures/rules established by the PSO. This might, for example, be by not following a treatment plan designed with their doctor (destruction of individual value) or by refusing to follow the rules for household recycling or by sabotaging those rules by fly-tipping (destruction of societal value). It can also be destroyed by a failure of the interaction between the public service user and public officials (e.g., the breakdown of trust between a patient and their doctor where treatment proves problematic).

1.7 Bringing Participation to Fruition

The preceding discussion has explored how participation has been framed and evolved within the five recent narratives of public service reform. An alternative narrative has subsequently been proposed – PSL. This integrates insights from PAM and SM&M to emphasize both participation as a core component of public service delivery and the creation of user and societal value as its core purpose. It also shifts the role of the public service users, including their needs, experiences and expectations, from the periphery to the heart of public service delivery. This marks an important departure in theorizing about participation in public services, where the transformative potential of public managers, professionals, and the stakeholder elite has traditionally been the emphasis. This is not to say that public service officials are unimportant or irrelevant. They are not – they have a key role to play. However, this role is predicated upon the value creation and co-creation activities of public service users and citizens – rather than vice versa. This latter element is the mainspring of participation and gives it a context and meaning. In order to achieve this requires a distinctive strategic orientation of public service managers.

1.8 A Strategic Orientation for Participation

Osborne et al. (2020) have explored how strategic orientation has long been recognized as important for organizational performance (Deshpande et al. 1993). It refers to an organization's capacity to create a culture of shared values and behaviour to underpin SPM. The literature focuses on three types of strategic orientation: cost-, market-, and customer-orientation. *Cost-orientation* has an internal focus, aimed at developing a culture of efficiency throughout a firm's internal value chain. *Competition-orientation* is the creation of a business culture across the firm that is oriented to market performance. *Customer-orientation* is the underlying organizational culture that facilitates the understanding of what constitutes 'value' for a firm's customers and how to embed such value at the heart of sustainable business practice. Whilst cost and market-orientation are necessary for organizational survival, it is customer-orientation that is an essential pre-condition of organizational effectiveness and the creation of customer value (Mediano and Ruz-Alba 2019).

For public services, both an internal cost-orientation and a competition-orientation were enduring features of the NPM. This enhanced the performance of individual PSOs, but at the cost of both the overall effectiveness of public service delivery ecosystems (McLaughlin et al. 2009) and their external effectiveness and value creation (Powell and Osborne 2020). Public Service Logic does not dismiss these orientations but rather argues that they need to be supplemented by a user and citizen orientation within an overall strategic orientation for public services. This is the only ways through which the benefits of citizen and user participation can be realized.

A user/citizen-orientation has four implications for public service delivery. First, it needs to be informed by an understanding of the centrality of the user/citizen to the delivery of effective and sustainable public services: it is only in the context of this orientation that cost and market information can be made sense of. Second, public service organizations need to evaluate internal resource and performance measures alone but rather to evaluate these in the context of external value creation and user needs. Third, it is only by embracing a user/citizen-orientation that PSOs can become truly sustainable as services, else they will continue to fail to be 'fit for purpose'. This requires that they adopt such an orientation to steer their strategic direction their role within public service reform trajectories. With such an orientation, citizen participation hence becomes recast not as an end in itself but rather as an intrinsic process at the heart of effective public service delivery to create value for both the individual and society (Grönroos 2019).

To fully realize the strategic orientation to participation articulated here, it is necessary to address three key challenges. First, the intrinsic and extrinsic processes of value-creation imply the skills and capacity of public service staff to understand and facilitate them. It is not so much a question of 'how to enable participation', but rather 'how to maximize the positive effects of the naturally occurring participation'. Such an approach is at odds with the product-dominant one that characterizes the prevailing NPM narrative and that posits participation as an add-on and constrained outcome rather than an intrinsic element of public service delivery (Loeffler and Bovaird 2016). This requires an orientation that understands external value creation as its end and participation as a means by which to achieve it.

Second, a value-creation approach to participation does not deny the challenges of enabling the extrinsic participative processes of public service delivery. The tensions of extrinsic participation common to the five discourses of public service reform discussed previously remain, particularly in terms of professional opposition to user-led services and partial or cosmetic forms of participation, the impact of professional power, and the skewing effect of elite capture of public services. Iterative waves of structural reforms have not been sufficient in overcoming these obstacles for public services, suggesting that enabling extrinsic forms of participation is dependent rather upon deeper cultural and strategic orientation changes for PSOs that seek to shift rather than ameliorate these structural and power imbalances. This is a challenging task but not impossible (Grönroos 2019).

Third, a value-creation strategic orientation to participation privileges working at the PSE level rather than focusing either upon the individual service user or citizen or the PSO alone. The dynamic interaction of the actors, structures, and processes within such ecosystems is central both to the effective governance of participation in public service delivery and to its contribution to the creation rather than destruction of individual and societal value (Osborne et al. 2022).

1.9 Conclusions: Implications for Practice

The alternate approach to participation presented here has five important implications for public service management. First, effective public service management requires an appreciation of the intrinsic processes of participation within the delivery of these services and the fundamental role of public service users and citizens during these processes. It requires to be consciously engaged with rather than allowing it to impact upon public service outcomes and value creation by default. Second, a pragmatic and sensitive approach to extrinsic forms of participation is necessary, that links the application of co-production and co-design in public service delivery to the individual and societal context of the needs that these services address. This is a task for both politicians and public service officials.

Third, value-creation through services can often require public service practitioners to balance value creation across different service users and stakeholders and/or between individual and societal value. This has significant implications for the role of participation, both intrinsic and extrinsic, in public service delivery. Fourth, embedding a value creation strategic orientation and its associated participative processes within public policy and public service management through cultural change is necessary to support the creation of value. As noted, such cultural change is a difficult but not impossible process to achieve and needs clear and unequivocal senior management leadership and support (Karp and Helg 2008). Further, such cultural change will need to address the endemic power imbalances discussed previously (Farr 2018). Finally, an effective strategic orientation requires embedding within a PSE approach to public service delivery. This will draw the essential links between participation in public service delivery by citizens and users and the creation of value for such users and for society. It will also provide a framework with both to mediate between the individual and society when their value agendas clash and to understand and ameliorate value destruction through public service delivery.

2 Motives, Incentives, and Tools of Citizens' Participation

Participation in public service delivery has been a recurrent element in the major public service reform narratives for a long time; thus, it has remained on the periphery of decision-making structures. The traditional model of public service delivery considered citizens as *users* or consumers who receive the services delivered to them (Alford 2009). This model, described in Section 1, needs to pay more attention to the intrinsic nature of service by which they necessarily play a role in the delivery process, as production and consumption as simultaneous processes and the service value is generated through the service experience (Osborne et al. 2013). It requires PSOs to adopt a strategic user/citizen orientation to steer the strategic direction of their role within public service reform trajectories. With such an orientation, citizen participation becomes an intrinsic process of public service delivery to create value for both the individual and society (Grönroos 2019).

Unlocking the participation principle at the base of PSL leads to a fundamental change in the relationship between the PSOs and its users, that citizens are no longer *passive receivers* of public services. Instead, they are seen as valuable participants in delivering public services (Osborne and Brown 2011b), situating their fundamental role in public service during these processes. Participation must be consciously engaged rather than allowing it to impact public service outcomes and value creation by default.

Recent research suggests a stable, long-term relationship between professionalized service providers and service users. All parties, including citizens, make substantial resource contributions (Bovaird 2007) to enhance the quantity and quality of service they receive (Brandsen and Honing 2016; Pestoff 2006). However, participation that links the application of co-design and co-production in public service delivery to the individual and societal context of the needs that these services address requires a pragmatic approach to extrinsic forms of participation. Therefore, understanding the motives, incentives, and tools to foster citizens' participation becomes central to this discussion of value-creation strategic orientation.

2.1 Reasons of Participation

Participation in public service delivery is not under the direct control of PSOs. Thus, they may initiate efforts that increase citizens' participation. Insights into how public service organizations may stimulate participation require understanding the reasons affecting citizens' participation. Existing literature offers two leading causes (Alford 2002; Jakobsen 2013; Porter 2012): ability and motivation.

Ability incorporates the theoretical assumption that citizens spend their time, knowledge, and efforts in the co-production of public services (Alford 2002; Brudney 1983; Percy 1984).

Citizens may have valuable knowledge about the service because they are policy experts or govern information about the service process. For example, they may be aware of the demand side of services and may contribute to the community's needs by articulating individual needs (Voorberg et al. 2015). They may have relevant competencies to deliver the service as skills to manage the co-production process (e.g., project management skills), skills to facilitate collaboration or leadership and ethical capacity (Van Eijk and Steen 2014). They may hold back from participating when they do not have the proper skill set or their time is lacking.

Thus, lifting the constraints on citizens' ability to co-produce by providing resources in the form of knowledge and materials necessary may enhance their level of co-production (Jakobsen 2013; Jakobsen and Andersen 2013). It may not be enough, as providing a context that supports co-production by enhancing the perception of public performance and how well the government involves citizens may influence their participation and the intensity of the efforts (Bovaird et al. 2016).

Motivation also drives participation in public service delivery. The theoretical discussion follows Alford's (2002) work that suggests individual self-motivation and prosocial (community) motivation stimulate citizens' engagement.

Self-motivation comes from the benefits that any individual may achieve in participating. The motivation may be intrinsic or extrinsic. Intrinsic motivation has been defined as the desire to expend efforts based on the interest in and enjoyment of an activity in and of itself, as proving to be capable of carrying out a task, or feeling part of a more significant collective (e.g., Amabile et al. 1994; Deci and Ryan 2010; Gagné and Deci 2005; Grant 2008). Self-motivation includes *emotional and psychosocial stimuli*, including personal interest, curiosity, and enthusiasm in the co-production initiative, as well as self-prestige and personal growth associated with fostering personal reputation and acquiring new skills (Asingizwe et al. 2020; Jennett et al. 2016; Kragh 2016; Larson et al. 2020; Rotman et al. 2014a); moreover, the sense of fulfilment from feeling like an active member of the society and feeling useful for the scientific community plays a role (Jennett et al. 2016; Kragh 2016; Rotman et al. 2014b).

On the contrary, extrinsic motivation is triggered by forces external to the co-production process and separable from it (e.g., Brief and Aldag 1977; Amabile 1993), and it refers to the desire to expend efforts to obtain an outside reward, as a private value from the service provided, or to avoid an outside punishment.

Prosocial motivation (or community motivation) moves the focus from one's self-interest to increased attention in the community. The motivation to engage in co-production for a community interest lies in contributing to a societal achievement or a worthwhile cause, or it must deal with the motivation to give back (Alford 2002; Grant 2007).

Self-interest and collective interest are not necessarily in contrast, as citizens may simultaneously be motivated by multiple factors (Brandsen and Helderman 2012). When a service is perceived as salient at the individual level (the citizen's perception of how a service affects themselves) or the community level (the importance of the services to a community), individuals will more likely consider active engagement by balancing between their ability (time, their investment of effort) and the effects of public service delivery (e.g., increased availability, quality, and efficiency) (Steen 2021).

On the contrary, citizens who need to learn how to co-produce are less likely to participate. Demonstrating how their ability and motivation can raise awareness towards citizens' participation (Thomsen and Jakobsen 2015). Thus, actual participation may require proper incentives and instruments.

2.2 Incentives of Participation

Citizens' participation in public service delivery has gained amplified popularity due to the affirmation of the new and pluralistic governance of service delivery, the scarcity of resources and fiscal constraints, and the evolving role of citizens and their communities (Agranoff and McGuire 2003; Nabatchi et al. 2017;

Osborne 2006; Osborne and Brown 2011a). Extrinsic co-production processes require deliberate and voluntary actions on the part of the citizens/service users in delivery of services (Osborne and Strokosch 2013). Their ability to contribute, in terms of time, knowledge, and expertise, is considered as relevant inputs for governments to mobilize resources for keeping public service provision maintainable (Bovaird 2007; Voorberg et al. 2018). Two categories of interventions are typically recognized as facilitators of citizens' ability: making the co-production task easier and enhancing the citizen's capacities to perform it (Alford 2002).

Digital technologies may make co-production tasks easier and stimulate citizens' participation. The development in information and communication technologies, the diffuse use of apps, social media, and mobile devices, and the new digital routines imposed by the pandemic restrictions offered new channels and modes through which citizens can contribute to data sharing about public services (e.g., providing the exact location of a pothole) and to the actual co-production of services (e.g., applying for education services or paying taxes online). Digital technologies are essential in simplifying co-production tasks (Alford 2009). In addition, online communication through social media may foster citizens' participation by appealing to social norms and nurturing mimicking actions to other persons in the network of the people engaging with the public service organizations. Technologies may be adopted to expand the current initiatives aimed at making participation easier, keeping into account the context of the stakeholders as digital poverty, digital illiteracy, and the digital divide (e.g., lack of the network infrastructure, lack of digital skills) that may increase inequalities among certain groups of citizens (e.g., migrants, the elderly, vulnerable people), as they may have fewer resources or inability to use technologies to get involved.

To enhance the ability to perform a co-production, public service organizations may provide information, advice, or training are typical examples that have a relevant role both at the point of access (Alford 2002; Jakobsen 2013) and during the interaction process (Prahalad and Ramaswany 2004). These tools may be advantageous for those lacking the knowledge necessary to contribute and benefit from the co-production process (Jakobsen and Andersen 2013). At the same time, how such knowledge and information is presented may enhance comprehension and steer participation (Porumbescu et al. 2017). Table 2 provides an overview of the incentives and tools used to foster co-production.

2.2.1 Incentives and Tools

Standard economic theories have traditionally relied on incentives and punishments to affect people's behaviour and even promote other-oriented acts like co-producing public services. Clear incentives could be a condition to mobilize

Table 2 Incentives and tools to participate.

Incentives of participation	Examples	
Mode of interaction	In person, mediated by web-based platforms; in hybrid modes.	Ampatzidou et al. (2018); Arienzo et al. (2021); Borghys et al. (2020); Compagnucci et al. (2021); Sorrentino, M., Sicilia, M. and Howlett, M. (2018); Vohland et al. (2021).
Communication	Guidelines, FAQs, tutorials, toolkits, or educational tools to learn from the experience. Consultations, surveys, quizzes, e-voting, crowdsourcing, hackathons, and gaming. Involvement of communities of interest or target groups.	Arienzo et al. (2021); August et al. (2019); Compagnucci et al. (2021); Dickinson et al. (2012); Jackson et al. (2020); Satorras et al. (2020); Vlachos et al. (2021); Golumbic et al. (2019); Roman et al. (2020).
Knowledge	Training; engagement of facilitators; sharing information about the public service and the participation activity.	Alford (2002); Jakobsen (2013); Jakobsen and Andersen (2013).
Intrinsic rewards	Provision of certificates, public acknowledgement, efforts' recognition, encouragement, and emphasis on the uniqueness of an individual's contribution.	Arienzo et al. (2021); Arnkil et al. (2010); Asingizwe et al. (2020); Compagnucci et al. (2021); Dickinson et al. (2012); Lakomy et al. (2020); Rotman et al. 2012; Vohland et al. (2021).
Material rewards	Monetary rewards, goods, or services.	Cooper and Culyer (1968); Alford (2009); Voorberg et al. (2018).
Sanctions	Monetary sanctions for non-participation.	Alford (2002).

citizens' effort and time in co-production. For instance, in the SM&M literature, monetary incentives play a substantial role in private co-creation. However, as Alford (2009) stresses, material rewards may fall short when applied to the public sector, and other intrinsic values might influence citizens' willingness to contribute to public service production. Several studies have investigated incentives affecting the motivation of citizens' participation in public service delivery, moving from Alford (2002, 2009).

Intrinsic Rewards: They may stimulate self-motivation. They are actions or behaviours that enhance satisfaction from feeling competent and autonomous or enjoying an activity. They resonate with individual fulfilment. They impact psychological satisfaction and include appreciation for participating and being involved in something they consider beneficial for themselves.

Solidary incentives: They stimulate participation to join collective actions. They are considered 'soft' incentives and include an emotional attachment or identification with a group. Citizens participate because they identify with the collective interests, share social ties with the community, and 'the rewards of associating with others, such as socialising, the sense of group membership and identification, being well regarded, and fun and conviviality' (Alford 2002: 35). Citizens participate either because of personal incentives such as their identity to a group, or their social norms, or the collective incentive of the intrinsic value of the collective good.

Normative appeals: They are explicit communications from the organization, or implicit meanings conveyed by organizational actions or behaviours, which signal identification with or support for valued social and moral ideals or principles.

Material rewards: They typically relate to tangible benefits as monetary rewards, goods, or services. For example, to increase the amount of available blood for transfusion purposes in the United Kingdom, some economists have argued in favour of introducing financial rewards for blood donors (e.g., Cooper and Culyer 1968). Monetary incentives are among those interventions that can be adopted to mobilize citizens' involvement in co-production, though some specific features of the public context may make them perform below expectations (Alford 2002, 2009). Indeed, PA scholars have shown that monetary incentives can often be ineffective in increasing individuals' performance within public organizations (Perry et al. 2009). The literature identifies three main reasons to explain such a failure (Bellé 2015). First, performance-related pay in the public sector are based on performance management practices (e.g., performance appraisal) that too often prove to be inadequate (Egger-Peitler 2007). Second, some institutional characteristics peculiar to public organizations make performance-related pay ineffective regardless of how well performance management practices are designed (Miller and Whitford 2007). Third, given the specific motivational traits of public employees, monetary incentives might produce unintended effects, different from those expected (Weibel et al. 2010). Studies on the crowding out effect of financial incentives on other motivation than extrinsic fall in this last explanation. To be effective, they have to be calibrated if implemented. Drawing on the concepts of social and economic exchange (Blau 1964), the risk of committing participation to an economic exchange is that the effort put in by citizens will then be limited to what is economically agreed. 'If they are willing to contribute time and effort to organisational purposes, they do so for their good reasons, which are much more complex than money or the avoidance of punishment' (Alford 2002: 45). This is particularly true for more complex co-productive tasks, where non-material rewards seem more effective, while material rewards shall be associated with more straightforward tasks (Alford 2009). Furthermore, the literature on PA shows that the effects of monetary rewards are marginal (Perry et al. 2009; Voorberg et al. 2018). Material incentives may also be hindered by the institutional constraints peculiar to the public sector that shall be applied to co-production. For example, budget constraints might make it unfeasible to offer large enough to be effective, irrespective of whether these bonuses are intended for public employees or co-producers. Citizens are not public employees, but they might share with the latter some motivational traits that go beyond personal utility maximization as a prosocial motivation (Alford 2002). In other words, conditions undermine the effectiveness of monetary incentives within public organizations in a co-production setting.

Sanctions: They usually are ineffective (or even counterproductive) in stimulating positive behaviours like co-producing as they convey the wrong message that this type of involvement is unpleasant and therefore to be avoided. They might increase compliance, but not willingness and overall engagement. Nevertheless, they 'elicit coproduction by facilitating the mobilization of other types of incentives' (Alford 2002: 43).

The effectiveness of each of these incentives depends on the form of co-production being promoted (Alford 2002). Individualistic initiatives are prompted more by material incentives, while collective ones are encouraged mostly by solidary incentives. Studies have investigated which incentives stimulate participation (Alford 2002; Andersen et al. 2017; Brudney 1983; Jackobsens 2013; Moseley et al. 2018; Voolberg et al. 2018). Their findings may suggest that citizens' participation in public service delivery is likely influenced by multiple factors, including the instruments used to engage them.

2.3 Instruments to Stimulate Participation

The incentives may be implemented with a range of instruments to stimulate participation. These instruments' use and effectiveness vary depending on the stage and the context in which they are utilized. Instruments may foster ability or motivation or both motives of participation.

2.3.1 Ability-Related Instruments

When engaging with citizens, one of the first elements that shape participation, and its future evolution relates to the definition of a physical and/or online space to facilitate participation (Schutz et al. 2019). This aspect deserves attention because physical spaces may restrict accessibility for those with limited mobility. Still, online participation may exclude specific groups of citizens who would be willing to participate but need more digital knowledge or resources. Thus, the selection of the space in which citizens participate in co-production also depends on the nature of the service and the target users involved, including a mix of physical and online meetings or ad hoc spaces for a different group of participants (Roman et al. 2020).

To unlock participation in co-production, some studies show engaging facilitators (Compagnucci et al. 2021; Roman et al. 2020; Vohland et al. 2021) to onboard citizens with practical aspects of the co-production and help them at the various stages favours their activities. Providing adequate supporting material improves individuals' ability to participate in service co-production. It may include information to be provided at the initial stages like protocols, guidelines, and tutorials on the tasks to be performed, toolkits and FAQs (Golumbic et al. 2019; Jackson et al. 2020; Vohland et al. 2021), or material that facilitates continuous involvement throughout the co-production, such as educational tools to learn from experience (Arienzo et al. 2021; August et al. 2019; Compagnucci et al. 2021; Dickinson et al. 2012; Golumbic et al. 2019; Satorras et al. 2020; Vlachos et al. 2021; Vohland et al. 2021).

Behavioural PA studies also proved that framing communication properly with citizens enhances or hinders their participation (Porumbescu et al. 2017). The information must be inclusive, understandable, and shared across subjects to facilitate understanding complex concepts (Vohland et al. 2021); creating a shared vocabulary may be an option (Bellandi et al. 2021).

When participation occurs in a digital space, like service platforms, they should be developed keeping in mind the users' experience, facilitating the accessibility and easiness of tasks (Asingizwe et al. 2020; Golumbic et al. 2019). Participation through social media is very useful in this framework as ways to facilitate participation, communication, and interaction (Compagnucci et al. 2021); examples include online consultations/surveys, quizzes, e-voting, crowdsourcing, blogging, or hackathons (Ampatzidou et al. 2018; Arienzo et al. 2021; August et al. 2019; Borghys et al. 2020; Compagnucci et al. 2021; Golumbic et al. 2019; Oksman and Kulju 2017; Selada 2017; Vallance et al. 2020; Vohland et al. 2021). Considering what already emerged when discussing about meetings, also in this case it is preferable to combine online and physical tools (Vohland et al. 2021).

2.3.2 Motivation-Related Tools

To foster motivation to participate, citizens must be convinced that their involvement in co-production activities have a substantial impact for themselves and the community (Vohland et al. 2021). Adopting tools to support the motivation incentives should be developed considering the concrete needs and interests of the potential co-producers, in light of their different backgrounds and levels of familiarity with the public services (Asingizwe et al. 2020).

In parallel, an important step to stimulate collective motivation is directly involving existing communities of interest, specific target groups, and individuals who have already participated in co-producing activities (Arienzo et al. 2021; Golumbic et al. 2019; Roman et al. 2020). Engagement requires constant and continuous support. During the initial engagement process, the definition of clear expectations for the citizens and the tasks they should perform is fundamental (Rotman et al. 2012; Vohland et al. 2021), as a certain level of expected effort can represent a barrier for those who are not particularly committed or do not have the proper ability. Several tools can be offered in ways or modular manners to facilitate participation with different levels of commitment (Fellnhofer 2017; Vohland et al. 2021). Recognition is an example of intrinsic reward; it allows individuals to realize they are valued and appreciated. High esteem by the other actors of the co-production process, as public service providers or the service's beneficiaries, may make citizens more enthusiastic about their participation in co-production. Training initiatives may both stimulate the ability to co-produce and build the basis for continuous participation, and it may also enhance the morale and motivation to co-produce. Another solid and recurrent motivating factor is the acknowledgement of an individual's contributions, which could be done through many different formats: certificates, public acknowledgement, efforts' recognition, encouragement, and emphasis on the uniqueness of an individual's contribution (Arienzo et al. 2021; Arnkil et al. 2010; Asingizwe et al. 2020; August et al. 2019; Dickinson et al. 2012; Lakomý et al. 2020; Rotman et al. 2012).

The physical settings and co-production environments may also facilitate motivation as they involve social interaction and can highly influence citizens' willingness to co-produce. Participation in decision-making may also stimulate participation, making citizens more committed towards their goals. To ensure continuous participation, a recurrent strategy employed relates to gamification (Arienzo et al. 2021; Vohland et al. 2021), such as using board games, role playing (Ampatzidou et al. 2018), and other elements of fun and play to promote friendly competition and stimulate virtuous cycles of task completion (August et al. 2019).

An essential element that must be taken into account throughout the co-production process is communication in terms of providing continuous updates. In the first case, it motivates citizens as they receive direct feedback about their work and thus become aware of the fact that their efforts are taken seriously (Arienzo et al. 2021; Asingizwe et al. 2021; August et al. 2019; Compagnucci et al. 2021; Golumbic et al. 2019; Roman et al. 2020; Vohland et al. 2021); also, giving information about the services' performance progress keeps the level of engagement high.

2.4 Implications for Theory and Practice

This section emphasizes the motives that foster the extrinsic participation of citizens in public service delivery. From a theoretical perspective, individual ability and motivation represent the main reasons to engage in co-production activities, often combined from one to the other (Alford 2002, 2009). Thus, public service organizations cannot control it. They can use incentives and supporting tools to stimulate citizens' participation. The practical choice depends on aspects connected to the nature of participation and the service itself. Identifying the proper set of tools depends on the context of co-production, the nature of the public service and the goals to achieve. The literature offers insights about some tools for engagement that appear to be among the most exploited. They are equally distributed among those expected to influence citizens' ability and motivation at all co-production stages.

Firstly, engagement requires proper modes of involvement. How citizens participate and interact (e.g., online, in person through meetings/workshops, and in person in the field) affects their ability to participate. The accessibility of technological devices to participate online could be a barrier for some categories of actors (e.g., seniors or less-educated individuals), while physical participation could pose similar issues for other segments of the population (e.g., people with physical disabilities). It also affects their motivation. The modes of involvement affect their sense of belonging (e.g., they feel part of a team that steers towards the same goal or rather an 'add-on' that provides resources).

Secondly, onboarding is essential. The support of facilitators or facilitating initiatives helps clarify citizens' doubts about how they can contribute and what is expected from them. Training may also be helpful to contextualize the co-production experience and increase participants' ability to contribute, particularly concerning the quality of their contributions and continuous engagement. Nevertheless, as for the presence of expert facilitators, this could require additional resources; that not every public service organization may provide.

Thirdly, material incentives, such as certificates or small financial rewards, may influence individual motivation and participation. Thus, empirical evidence shows mixed results (Voorberg et al. 2018). Deciding to invest in these tools represents a choice that might vary depending on specific categories of participants.

Thus, this section focuses primarily on the citizens' perspective. Other actors are crucial in explaining public service provision and its value starting from public service professionals.

The imperative to understand the motivation of public service professionals in the co-creation of services is underscored by a multitude of factors. These elements encompass the following. Firstly, the public service motivation of civil servants. The literature suggests that they may be extrinsically and intrinsically motivated (Ritz et al. 2016), but of them especially the professionals coming from the private sector usually have a prosocial motivation and want to make a societal impact (Mergel, Bellè, and Nasi 2021). Secondly, the cultivation of leaders and champions for public service delivery, both within the frontline staff and senior management ranks is important to effectively engage in the service co-production (Brewer and Selden 2000). Thirdly, the formulation and implementation of institutional plans that explicitly incorporate or acknowledge the role of citizen and public engagement (Burby 2003). Each of these components serves to bolster the motivation of public service professionals by offering tangible avenues for meaningful involvement and recognition within the co-creation process. Consequently, a concerted focus on motivation emerges as a fundamental imperative in fostering a conducive environment for effective collaboration and innovation in public service provision (Osborne et al. 2021).

This is an area that, along with others, requires further investigation under the PSL approach. From a PSL perspective, studies on participation have focused on stimulating citizens' participation by looking at the dyadic relationship between PSOs and citizens rather than situating it within complex and interactive *service ecosystems*, comprising the key actors and processes of value creation as well as societal, institutional values, rules, and social norms (Akaka and Schau 2019). We argue that the dynamic behaviour of actors within the ecosystem may influence the effects of incentives. It requires investigation under the most appropriate framing of the delivery of public services at the ecosystem level.

In addition, whether participation in public service delivery contributes to value-creation remains rather normative than a positive affirmation (Cui and Osborne 2023a). We advocate more research in this domain to map and depict if and how participation affects the elements of value creation across in public services.

3 Public Service Ecosystems and Participation

Section 2 discusses how PAM theory has been challenged in the twenty-first century, leading to a new paradigm of engagement and participation of citizens and other actors in public service delivery. The dominant paradigm, the NPM, grounded in the manufacturing logic of public services, focused on intra-organizational efficiency (Radnor et al. 2016), has become subject to widespread critiques. Among the criticisms, one relates to its provider–user relationships based on a dyadic relationship that omits the societal values and social norms that shape the dynamic public service processes where citizens, public managers, users, PSOs, and the local community interact and participation. Consequently, alternative discourses have arisen with insights from SM&M into PAM and focus on value creation as the natural *purpose* of public services. This paradigm has reoriented PAM in two respects and is incorporated into the PSL (Osborne 2021; Osborne et al. 2013). It has shifted its focus to the *value* that the use/consumption of services generates, and it elevates the service as the *value creation process* (Grönroos 2017; Vargo et al. 2017).

In this context, a value-creation strategic orientation to participation privileges works at the PSE level rather than focusing on the individual service user, a citizen, or the PSO alone. The PSE positions public service value creation not as the purview of the PSO providing the service but instead as occurring within complex and interactive *service dynamics*, comprising the key actors and processes of value creation as well as societal, institutional values, rules, and social norms (Akaka and Schau 2019).

The dynamic interaction of the actors, processes, and technologies within such ecosystems is central to the effective governance of participation in public service delivery and its contribution to the creation rather than destruction of individual and societal value (Cui and Osborne 2023b; Osborne et al. 2022). In this section, we discuss the concept of a PSE to situate participation in a dynamic relationship among its actors.

3.1 The Public Service Ecosystem

The growing consensus that traditional bureaucratic models of public service delivery are no longer adequate to meet the complex and rapidly evolving needs of citizens has led many organizations towards a more holistic, ecosystem-based approach to public service delivery that engages citizens more directly and holistic-ally. This shift is based on the recognition that PSEs are complex. These dynamic systems involve multiple stakeholders, including government agencies, non-profit organizations, private sector actors, and the citizens who use their services.

Public service ecosystem-based approach to service delivery is essential for ensuring that public services are effective, efficient, and responsive to the needs of citizens. This is because such an approach recognizes the complex inter-dependencies between the various actors and stakeholders involved in deliver-ing public services and the importance of engaging citizens more directly and effectively in designing, implementing, and evaluating these services. The concept of the 'service ecosystem' was initially developed in the work of Vargo and his colleagues (2017) on the 'service-dominant logic' approach to SM&M. It drew upon the analogy to ecosystems within the ecological literature. Service ecosystems have subsequently become the front line of SM&M theory development, integrating institutional and user concerns with the service level (e.g., Mustak and Ple 2020; Vink et al. 2021).

Systemic approaches to public service delivery, such as the 'Production of Welfare' model of social care (Knapp 1984), have also long been a preoccupation of the PAM research community, as has a context (Pollitt 2013). The PSE approach goes further, however. It explores both context and system and the interactions of the institutional, service, and individual levels of public service delivery. Trischler and Charles (2019), for example, have described it pre-cisely as a unifying framework through which to understand the complexities of public service delivery and value creation at the societal, service, and individual levels. Value is not something created in isolation by public service users. Rather it is nested within overlapping and interacting relationships within the PSE.

This argument was amplified further by Petrescu (2019) and Strokosch and Osborne (2020), who contribute to the notion of the PSE within PSL as an essential perspective on public service delivery. They argue that the ecosystem introduces a relational model of public service in which value is shaped by the interplay between all of the dimensions of the ecosystem, and not least by the wider societal context and the values that underpin it.

In other words, PSEs are complex networks of interdependent entities and actors that collaborate to provide public services. Kinder et al. (2020, 2022) have argued that PSEs have now replaced networks as the most persuasive framework for understanding public service delivery, whilst Rossi and Tuurnas (2021) have subsequently argued that PSEs reveal the complexity of value creation conflicts. They encompass a wide range of actors, including public service and non-profit organizations, firms, associations of users, community groups, and individuals. They involuntary and actively collaborate to provide public services and are characterized by a foundation of shared values. Studies of PSEs can now be found exploring such diverse issues as digital public services and Big Data (Cordella and Peletti 2019), smart cities (Ciasullo et al. 2020), value destruction within public services (Engen et al. 2021; Cui and Osborne 2023b), and public service responses to the Covid-19 pandemic (Brodie et al. 2021). It has also been integrated into formal PAM theory through the development of PSL (Osborne 2021), focusing on the elements of value in a public service context (Osborne et al. 2021).

In turn, the engagement of all actors and stakeholders in the PSE processes are essential for their success. Participation may be shaped in many ways, including consultation, co-creation, and collaboration, and it may occur at different stages of the process, from commission, co-design, co-production, and co-evaluation (Nabatchi et al. 2017). Through stakeholder engagement, the PSE mobilizes skills, knowledge, and resources of the diverse actors and stakeholders to co-create services that generate value for the needs of the individuals and the community (Osborne 2021; Osborne et al. 2022).

3.2 Public Service Ecosystems and Stakeholders' Participation

Public service ecosystems and participation are closely related. The value generated by the PSE processes is dependent upon the involvement of citizens and other stakeholders (Cui and Osborne 2023a; Osborne et al. 2022). Participation is important for multiple actors in the PSE, not only the identified service user. Citizens who are not users of public service can also accrue value, perhaps through a role as a volunteer or carer in a public service, but it can also be through the way that participation in public service delivery enables societal value, such as social inclusion or environmental enhancement (Musso et al. 2019). Individual and societal values are not always congruent and can sometimes conflict (Benington 2011). Further, even individuals who are not citizens can accrue value through participation in public service delivery – such as tourists (Soszyński et al. 2018) or asylum seekers (Strokosch and Osborne 2016).

Participation may occur in different manners, ranging from engaging in advocacy activities to providing feedback, volunteering, and actively contributing to the service delivery processes. In addition, it may foster transparency, accountability, and responsiveness, which are critical components of effective governance (Porumbescu et al. 2017; Tria et al. 2012). In turn, stakeholder engagement can build trust and legitimacy by contributing to the decision-making and delivery processes and aligning expectations about services with their actual design (OECD 2017).

However, participation requires a commitment to constant communication and continuous collaboration. This includes establishing clear channels for a collaborative effort, tools to facilitate engagement and assessing its impact (Sørensen and Torfing 2011).

Public service ecosystems involve various public and private entities providing services and infrastructure to meet the needs of citizens, businesses, and other organizations. Personal, social, and institutional factors can influence participation in PSEs.

There are several determinants of engagement in PSEs, which include individual factors, social factors, and institutional factors. These determinants can vary depending on the context and the specific PSE (Nabatchi and Leighninger 2015).

Individual factors are concerned with the elements that may influence the perception of value creation/destruction for citizens, service users, and all other key stakeholders who are not service users but who accrue value from the public service delivery process in relation to their needs, expectations, and experiences. They include personal characteristics such as social or economic interests. Individual antecedents of participation may also be similar to those discussed in Section 2. Thus, more in general, people with different socioeconomic backgrounds may have different levels of participation in PSEs (Emerson et al. 2012). For instance, individuals with lower income and education levels may be less likely to participate in civic activities, such as voting or volunteering, due to financial constraints, lack of competencies or lack of information. Age, gender, race, and ethnicity can all affect participation in PSEs. For instance, younger people tend to be less involved in traditional civic activities, such as voting, but are more likely to participate in online civic activities, such as signing petitions or joining online groups. People with significant cognitive impairments and/or social vulnerabilities may also be less likely to participate in collaborative initiatives (Skarli 2021).

Social factors that influence stakeholders' engagement include social norms, ideologies, and trust in institutions. Social norms, such as the expectation to participate in public life, can motivate stakeholders to engage in PSEs. Trust in government and other stakeholders is also critical for engagement, as it can foster a sense of legitimacy and accountability. People who have more trust in government are more likely to participate in civic activities and are more willing to engage with public institutions. Social networks, such as community organizations and civil society groups, can provide citizens with a sense of community and facilitate their engagement in PSEs. In addition, the political culture and social capital of a community may impact participation in PSEs. In some countries, people have a strong tradition of participating in civic activities and engaging with public institutions, while in others, there is a more cynical attitude toward government and public services (Putnam 2000).

Institutional factors may also foster or hinder participation. They include the design of PSEs, the technologies adopted, and the quality of communication and information. Public service ecosystems that are designed to be inclusive and participatory are more likely to engage citizens effectively. The use of technology, such as online platforms, can make it easier to access information about public services, participate in online forums, and engage with government agencies. On the other hand, the digital divide and lack of digital literacy can limit access to these resources, particularly for disadvantaged groups. Moreover, PSEs that prioritize ongoing communication and provide citizens with quality information are more likely to foster engagement.

Finally, engagement may be fostered to promote social cohesion and building resilient communities. When citizens are engaged in PSEs, they can connect with one another and work collaboratively to address shared challenges (Nasi and Choi 2023). This can help to build social networks and strengthen the fabric of communities, leading to more cohesive and resilient societies.

The active engagement of the actors of PSEs is critical for promoting effective, efficient, and responsive public services, building trust and legitimacy in public institutions, and fostering resilient and cohesive communities. One key element of a PSE-based approach is the need to engage citizens and other stakeholders in co-creation and co-design of public services. This involves working with citizens to identify their needs and preferences, co-designing services that meet these needs, and co-evaluating the effectiveness of these services. By engaging citizens in this way, public service providers can ensure that services are more responsive to the needs of citizens and that services are delivered in a meaningful and relevant way.

Another important aspect of engaging citizens in PSEs is the need to promote transparency and accountability in the delivery of public services. This involves ensuring that citizens have access to information about the services they receive, how they are delivered, and how they are evaluated. It also involves ensuring that citizens have a voice in the design, implementation, and evaluation of these services, and that they are able to hold public service providers accountable for their actions.

3.3 Implications for Theory and Practice

Engaging stakeholders in PSEs is essential for ensuring that public services are effective, efficient, and responsive to the needs of citizens. By recognizing the complex interdependencies between the various actors and stakeholders involved in the delivery of public services, and by promoting transparency and accountability in the delivery of these services, we can ensure that public services are delivered in a way that is meaningful and relevant to the lives of citizens. An active engagement of stakeholders in the design, implementation, and evaluation of public services, we can ensure that these services are delivered in a way that is more effective, efficient, and responsive to the needs of citizens.

To advance theory and practice, several domains of study and empirical investigations should be considered.

Firstly, moving from the existing knowledge on motives of participation and engagement, researchers and practitioners should aim to understand the factors that influence citizens and other stakeholders' decisions to participate in PSEs (Jilke and Van Ryzin 2020). Stakeholders in PSEs are not just individuals; their motives to participate may differ from those described in Section 3. An in-depth assessment of what motivates stakeholders to get engaged is paramount to advance our understanding of the functioning of PSEs. This could involve examining the dynamic role of individual, social, and institutional factors that drive or impede participation, adopting proper methods of investigation.

Consequently, continuous and active engagement requires a proper governance and the identification of effective strategies for increasing participation (Sørensen and Torfing 2021). Once researchers understand what motivates stakeholders to participate, they can then focus on developing effective strategies for increasing participation.

This might involve testing different types of incentives, improving the stakeholders' experience of public service platforms, or leveraging mixed strategies to encourage more people to get involved. In addition, the role of emerging technologies in PSEs should also be explored. As new technologies continue to emerge, they are likely to impact how PSEs are designed and operated significantly. Researchers should therefore investigate the potential benefits and challenges associated with integrating emerging technologies such as blockchain, artificial intelligence, and the Internet of Things (Bright and Margetts 2018; Meijer and Thaens 2018).

Lastly, current research on participation and the PSE relies on the normative assumption that the success of PSEs depends on the ability of all its actors to deliver effective and efficient services to the public. However, it remains to be seen how value is created through the participation and dynamic relationship among the PSE's actors, processes, and structures.

4 Citizens and Value Creation

Previous sections have elaborated the PSL. We began by reviewing the evolving recognitions of citizens' role in public services: a shift from citizens as simply voters and consumers to citizens as problem solvers and co-creators of value. A distinguishment has been made particularly between two streams of co-production theory: an *efficiency* perspective viewing citizens' co-production as something 'added into' service planning and production; and a *service* perspective viewing citizens' co-production as an essential and inalienable core component of service delivery (Osborne et al. 2016).

The latter has led to the establishment of PSL theory in recent years, a theory that attempts to integrate insights from SM&M together with those in PA (Osborne et al. 2013). It understands public service as 'service' – the process of 'doing something for someone' (Vargo and Lusch 2008); rather than 'manufacturing' – producing impersonal goods according to technical specifications. Public Service Logic proponents hence articulated that the authentic *value*, about how public services make changes, can only be created and arbitrated by users during their consumption and contextualization (Osborne 2020). The latest work in PSL has argued that such value creation can take different forms and that this takes place within a dynamic PSE (Osborne et al. 2022). The PSE situates value creation in a multi-level nested social structure, comprising the key actors and processes of value creation, as well as societal and institutional values and rules (Petrescu 2019).

This section will further explore how citizen participation can create value within a PSE context. It is a continuation of Sections 4 and 5, which respectively discussed citizen's motivations to engage in public service design/delivery and how they co-produce the interactive, complex, and self-sustained service ecosystem. This section will present two important arguments. First, citizens are the final arbiters of value creation; and they create value through their participation in service design, delivery, and consumption. Furthermore, such participation is not isolated and requires the support of multiple stakeholders, institutions, and technologies. Second, once poorly organized, participation can result in 'value destruction', making our society and service users' lives worse (Engen et al. 2021).

In this section, we will refer to some empirical evidence to exemplify our theoretical arguments. This evidence, collected from our qualitative research on the Covid-19 vaccination programme in Scotland over 2021–2022, aims to uncover the complicated pro-/anti-vaccination behaviours and their underlying reasons.

4.1 Actor, Institution, and Technology

This section will describe the process of value creation in public service design, delivery, and consumption phases. As Section 3 elaborated, the pursuit of value creation fundamentally catalyses citizens to participate in a PSE (Section 4), in which citizens and groups interact and further co-create value. To explain this complex citizen participation process, we will first explain the context of public services, and then elucidate the necessary actors, institutions, and technologies within this context.

4.1.1 Setting the Scene for Value Creation in Public Services

Service-dominant logic researchers from SM&M articulate 'value' as 'the positively or negatively valenced change in well-being or viability of a particular system/actor' (Vargo and Lusch 2018: 740). Such value is subjectively determined by users and is always heterogeneous (multiple value pursuits in one public service process), phenomenological (different users create different value), and experiential (different users create value based on their own life experiences) (Akaka and Schau 2019). Furthermore, SDL researchers maintain that the traditional demarcation between 'services' and 'goods' is artificial – both are 'service-delivery vehicles' and do not have intrinsic value. It is how such services/goods are utilized by a customer that creates value, a process known as 'value-in-use' (Vargo and Lusch 2008).

Vargo et al. (2017) subsequently added that 'value-in-use' alone does not explain the full picture of how value is added to customers' lives. They argued that consumers are embedded within their own social systems and equipped with their own beliefs and values. They argued that value could not be created independently through service encounters and consumptions, since customers are embedded within their own social systems. It is thus important to explore the context of customers – their needs, expectations, prior experiences, and social milieu. This is captured by the concept of 'value-in-context'.

The concepts of value-in-use and value-in-context measure the extent to which a service impacts upon the needs of a service user, within the setting of their own life experiences (Grönroos 2017). Grönroos and Voima (2013) have suggested a process model situate value creation across three interlinked spheres. As shown in Figure 1, there are provider sphere (real value has not been generated, but service providers prepare/produce service offerings, though which delivering the propositions and promises of value), joint sphere (value can be created in direct service encounters and consumption), and user sphere (value can be created by users in the context of their expectations and experiences).

This process model conceptualizes the value creation process in businesses and private sector services. Notably, it is an inherently commercial model: businesses support the value creation of their customers in the hope that

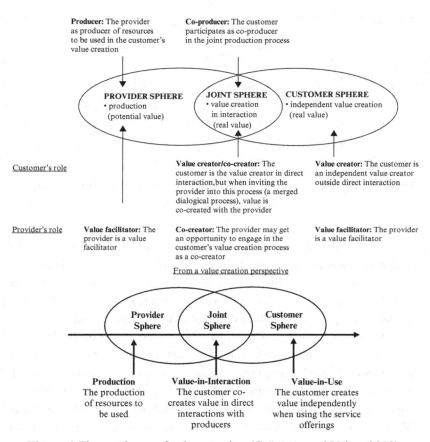

Figure 1 Three spheres of value creation (Grönroos and Voima 2013).

customers return to visit their businesses, through which to obtain sustained business growth (Osborne et al. 2022). However, value creation in public services is significantly different. This shows in the distinctive ownership of public and third sectors. Furthermore, public services normally have multiple users and other stakeholders (such as users' family and friends, public service staff, and other citizens), who have different subjective perceptions of value (e.g., Powell and Osborne 2020; Hardyman et al. 2019). Besides, public service users are not always willing. They can be required (such as school children), coerced (such as prison inmates), and unconscious (such as adults with dementia) (Alford 2016).

The recent study by Osborne, Nasi, and Powell (2021) offers a holistic model to explain the value creation process in public services. This model has extended the relevant discourse in SM&M in two aspects. First, it has emphasized the need to 'explore *both* the production and the use/consumption of

Citizens'	Process			
participation in	Production		Consumption	
public service	Co-design	Co-production	Co-experience	Co-construction
provision				
Citizens' role	Co-design of services	Co-management and co-delivery	Creating the positive/negative experience of a public service through value in context	Creating the effect/impact of a public service upon their life (and vice versa) through value in use

Figure 2 The processes of value creation for public services (modified from Osborne et al. 2021).

public services in order to [fully] understand value creation' (8). The use/consumption process can enable the realization of value-in-use and/or value-in-context, while in the public service context, service production is another essential process through which value can be created. As shown in Figure 2, this production process is further differentiated into two explicit processes: co-design and co-production. Co-design refers to the involvement of citizens and groups in the design stage of public services. There is increasing evidence from both SM&M and PA demonstrating that co-design is a promising approach to enhancing learning, subsequently leading to service innovation and improved service experiences (e.g., Steen et al. 2011; Trischeler et al. 2018; Trischeler et al. 2019). Co-production concerns the conscious engagement of citizens (not only direct users but also can include other citizen groups such as through volunteering) in the delivery of public services. This process can contribute to the enhanced service outcome, as well as the development of co-producers' capacity for the future (Tuurnas et al. 2015).

As Osborne et al. (2021) highlighted, service co-design and co-production are not isolated stages in public service delivery. Rather, they have suggested understanding value creation 'as an interactive cluster of production and use/consumption processes' (8).

Second, the process model offered by Osborne et al. (2021) also suggests that public services do not only add value to individual citizens but also need to add value to the society as a whole.[1] This argument is associated with the important debate about PV, evolved from the work of Moore (1995), who underlined public managers' responsibility for creating something 'substantively valuable

---

[1] It is valuable to note that, a few studies have started to discuss the creation of 'public value' in private sectors and businesses from a comparative perspective between the public value concept with adjacent ones such as corporate CSR. See, for instance, Meynhardt and Jasinenko (2020).

for the society' (71). Public Value debate has latterly evolved into a cluster of theories regarding its substances and creation (e.g., Stoker 2006; Bozeman 2007; Bryson et al. 2017). Three conceptualizations have gradually emerged, respectively understanding PV from 'what the public values', 'what adding to the public sphere', and 'what satisfying widely-accepted public values criteria' (Cui and Osborne 2023a). Despite its conceptual ambiguity and heterogeneity, PV theory was regarded as an important theory that sought to shift the practice and research in PA from the preoccupation with efficiency and markets to the public services' external impacts on society (O'Flynn 2021). The research of PSL has evolved alongside the discourse on PV. However, whilst PV theory solely focuses on value creation at the societal level, PSL researchers explore both public and private value and their interactions.

Integrating the process model with the PSE (Osborne et al. 2022; Vargo and Lusch 2016), Figure 3 demonstrates the context of value creation in public services in a unifying framework. Vertically, it aggregates four overlapping system layers. The macro-level represents the institutional arrangements that legitimate value creation in society. The meso-level and the micro-level respectively refer to the organizational actors and their networks/rules, and the individual actors, including users, individual providers, and other stakeholders. Individual actors' behaviours are further shaped by their beliefs and values at the sub-micro level.

Horizontally, public service delivery takes place between the meso- and micro-levels. This delivery process is where citizen participation takes place. This participation includes the procedures when providers (representing different public service organizations), users, and other key stakeholders interact in a network to co-design and co-produce public services. It also includes service consumption (including co-experience and co-construction) by users independently. The societal values/norms at the Macro-level regulate this delivery

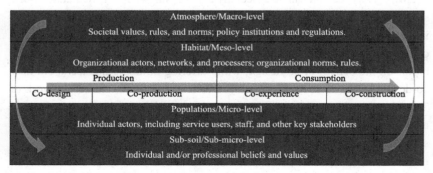

Figure 3 The context of value creation in public services.

process. These macro-level societal values/norms validate 'what types of value are socially desirable and what public service delivery processes are permissible' (Osborne et al. 2022: 5).

4.1.2 Actors and their Institutional/Technological Support

Figure 3 sets the scene for the value creation in public services. In this complex environment, there are three types of essential actors: public service designers, producers, and users. Citizens can participate by playing these roles, and/or a combination of different roles.

Public Service Designers: They refer to the actors who are involved in a reflective practice in which they 'cocreating problems and solutions in an exploratory, iterative process in which problems and solutions co-evolve' (Kimbell 2011: 42). Conventionally, service designers are restricted to professionals and experts (e.g., Schön 1987). In a public service setting, these professions and experts are expected to collaborate with governments to 'develop or alter value propositions' (Røhnebæk et al. 2024: 4). However, this expert-driven idea has recently been challenged by the introduction of the concept 'service co-design'. The latter refers to 'a collective activity of a team with members from different backgrounds and interests' (Trischler et al. 2019: 1595).

Citizens can act as co-designers for public services following this 'service co-design' idea. They can contribute as a part of the design team as 'experts of their experience' (Sanders and Stappers 2008). Increasing empirical studies have demonstrated that this contribution is important since this allows the translation of user knowledge into new service ideas and configuration of resources which are more innovative and better address users' needs (Chang and Taylor 2016; Trischler et al. 2018). Besides, citizens' involvement is argued to facilitate the service implementation by enhancing 'citizens experience and interact with social problems, services, and programmes' (Clarke and Craft 2018: 8).

However, co-design can be especially challenging when it is related to public service projects dealing with sensitive or less engaging topics, and projects involving vulnerable user groups (e.g., deprived communities, adults with dementia) (e.g., Dietrich et al. 2017). Most existing studies, however, only report on the benefit of co-design, while offering limited guidance about how co-design activities should be deployed. One exemption is the recent work of Trischler, Dietrich, and Rundle-Thiele (2019), which has articulated the importance of institutions and policies to support (1) recruiting and sensitizing suitable service users, (2) conditions enabling users to co-design ideas, and (3) requirements for implementation of user-driven ideas. Additionally, the studies of Osborne et al. (2022) and Trischler and Westman-Trischler (2022) have discussed co-design in the age of digitalization. Differentiated from prior research that mainly argued for the positive influence of the virtual approach (Kennedy et al. 2021), they argued that virtual co-design has both strengths and weaknesses, which thereby requires an elaborated institutional arrangement.

Public Service Producers: They refer to the actors who are voluntarily or involuntarily involved in managing and delivering public services. Governments and public sectors are traditional public service producers, while citizens can also act as producers – a point we have fully amplified in Section 2.

Our recent research on the Scottish Covid-19 vaccination programme shows that large public service projects usually need multiple service providers from public, private, third sectors, and different citizen groups. These providers interacted based on the pre-existed network, for instance, the 'Voluntary Health Scotland (VHS)', which allows the value pursuits of different minority groups can be considered in the programme delivery. The CEO of VHS explained that:

> We are quite a broad church. We are a network and membership body of different voluntary organizations. I suppose the shared interest across our network is in health inequality. Most of the organizations in our network provide direct services to different client groups. (Interview – 31/25/2022)

Notably, when citizens voluntarily participate in public service production, value can be created directly in its own right, shown as, for example, the development of personal skills, improved personal confidence, and a sense of satisfaction and gain. A large number of respondents from our recent vaccination research and community-level carbon reduction research have corroborated this point.

Citizens' co-production can result in the proactive creation of alternative services and service innovation. Gofen (2015) maintained that public service provision 'reflects different assumptions regarding the relationship between individual citizens and the state' (405). Due to the 'dissatisfaction', citizens can occasionally practice noncompliance with existing services and initiate an alternative form of services, namely 'entrepreneurial exit'. This entrepreneurial role of citizens needs to be protected and guided by positive and supporting institutional and policy design (Kleinhans 2017). Digital technologies are welcomed in the co-production of public services. However, there is no reason to assume that digital technology will always encourage co-production. In fact, it can be used to exclude and bypass citizens' engagement (Lember et al. 2019).

Public Service Users: They refer to the consumers of public services who create authentic 'value' by integrating resources from many different sources within their different life-worlds. This is the intrinsic role that citizens can play to participate in public services. According to PSL theory, this consumption/contextualization process cannot be influenced by public service providers directly.

Instead, 'it is the service users who decides what resources she/he integrates into her/his value creation process' (Trischler and Westman-Trischler 2022: 1256), to solve their problems and/or achieve their personal development goals. This resource integration and value creation processes are rooted in users' individual values and beliefs at the sub-micro level. Service providers can only facilitate this individual-level value creation process through, for example, ensuring users' access to resources and directing their resource use (Hardyman et al. 2019). This relies on the assemblages of interdependent institutions – 'human devised rules, norms, and beliefs that enable and constrain actions and make social life predictable and meaningful' (Vargo and Lusch 2016: 11).

Public policies are a typical type of institution. As the outcome of political debate, policies offer a codification of the societal values and beliefs embedded within public services. They have no value in their own right. Rather they are a series of aspirations that may, or may not, be achieved by implementation/ enactment through public services (Osborne, Cucciniello, and Cui, in-print). These institutions and policies can provide users with effective guidance, which, arguably, enables users to accomplish resource integration and value creation properly and efficiently under their time and cognitive constraints. Meanwhile, institutions also form the structure of the service ecosystem and regulate relationships (Vargo and Lusch 2016).

Our Covid-19 vaccination research identified and analysed forty-five signifi-cant public policies. This documentary analysis revealed how the institutional focuses of the Covid-19 vaccination programme have evolved in Scotland – from an initial fixation on the deployment speed/scale to growing considerations given to the inclusiveness and equity issues. It also illustrates how the policy design and implementation were influenced by the changes in the external institutional environment. For example, given the rapid spread of Covid-19, the equal focus on both doses at the beginning of the programme was quickly replaced by a concentration on the first dose. These policies have steered the implementation of vaccination programme and guided individual citizens' behaviours.

Taken together, Table 3 summarizes three types of role that citizens can plan, and the institutional/technological support required. It needs to clarify that co-designers, co-producers, and users are three main actors. However, there are other stakeholders, such as social care agencies and users' families and friends. Research about their roles in value creation is emerging (e.g., Powell et al. 2019).

4.2 Value Destruction

The Section 4.1 discussed the context and process of value creation, as well as the actors, institutions and technologies within this context. However, citizen

Table 3 Actors, institutions, and technologies in value creation.

Actors	Institutional support	Technological support
Co-designers: *Citizens can act as the 'experts of their experience'*	Institutions to facilitate the recruiting and sensitizing of suitable users into co-design, and secure the implementation of user-driven ideas.	Digital technologies and virtual environments that can reduce the threshold of users' involvement and facilitate the process of co-design.
Co-producers: *Citizens can co-produce public services and accrue value directly*	Institutions to establish and maintain the collaboration network, encourage innovation, and protect the entrepreneurial role of citizens.	Technologies that facilitate communication, negotiation, and co-production.
Users and resource integrators: *Citizens create value independently*	Institutional arrangement and infrastructure that can provide users with effective guidance and form the structure of service ecosystems.	Technology as a type of resources being used directly to help value creation, and as an approach facilitating resource access, communication, processing, and actuation.

participation in public services does not always create value. Rather, it can destroy value and make users' lives and society worse. This is termed 'value destruction' – the dark side of value creation. This section will first conceptualize value destruction with reference to both SM&M and PA literature. Then, it will explain the situations where participation results in value destruction

4.2.1 Unpacking the Concept of Value Destruction

The research on value destruction in SM&M is still embryonic. It emerged from Plé and Chumpitaz Cáceres (2010), who articulated that prior value co-creation research has a fixation on the service interaction associated with positive processes and outcomes. This 'optimistic' view constrains the exploration of the adverse possibility of 'value co-destruction'. They subsequently defined value co-destruction as:

> An interactional process between service systems that results in a decline in at least one of the system's well-being. (431)

Plé and Chumpitaz Cáceres (2010) further articulated that the accidental or intentional 'misuse' of resources is the trigger for value co-destruction. As different participants in a service situation have their own value expectations, value co-destruction occurs when there are discrepancies between parties regarding expectations of appropriate resource-usage behaviour. To overcome value co-destruction, they suggested enhancing communication and the training and empowering of frontline service providers. Subsequent empirical research following this line of inquiry has added that the accidental misuse of resources is the most common form of value co-destruction (e.g., Vafeas et al. 2016).

In comparison, the research of Echeverri and Skålén (2011) represents another stream of value co-destruction research in the SM&M. They first argued for a dynamic way to explore value formation – viewing value co-creation and co-destruction in a *reciprocal* relationship. Consequently, they suggested four types of value formation: reinforcing value co-creation, recovery value co-formation, reductive value co-formation, and reinforcing value co-destruction. This argument is further amplified by the later research of Laamanen and Skålén (2015). They conceptualized value co-creation as a collective action and maintained that within such action, conflicts and discordance inherently exist and remain inevitable.

Furthermore, Echeverri and Skålén (2011) advocated exploring value co-destruction in a broader context: not only in the dyadic relationships between service providers and users, but associated with complex and interactive service systems where the uneasy relationships between participants account for the negative value results. Their subsequent empirical analysis has examined the interaction between firms and their brand communities (Skålén et al. 2015a). Drawing upon a netnographic study of an online brand community platform, they suggested that value can be co-created when diverse actors' practices align and co-destructed when their practices misalign. They further proposed three realignment strategies, including compliance (reaffirming the need to comply with established rules), interpretation (enhanced dialogue), and orientation (reorienting the purpose of a practice). Similarly, Skålén's et al. (2015b) went beyond the traditional private service field to explore how activists using ICT tools to transform service systems during the Arab Spring. They revealed how the latent or overt conflicts between activists and regimes could result in value creation or destruction under different circumstances.

The latest research by Echeverri and Skålén (2021) provides a critical review of value co-destruction research in SM&M. They argued that resource misuse research fails to reveal the dynamic social mechanisms inherent in the interactive nature of value co-destruction. They also attempted to make a differentiation between value co-destruction and its adjacent concepts, such as consumer exploitation and value failure.

This expanding SM&M discourse on value co-destruction has recently spread into the PA literature. Järvi et al. (2018; see also Laud et al. 2019) developed this discourse by differentiating between value destruction (as a result of poor service delivery and management) and value co-destruction (as a result of the failure of interactions between public service providers, users and other actors). With the introduction of the PSL, emerging studies have started to explore the dynamics of value destruction in public services (e.g., Engen et al. 2021; Espersson and Westrup 2020; Straussman 2022). As Cui and Osborne (2023a) summarized, these studies have identified three primary reasons for value destruction: (1) power asymmetries between public service providers and users; (2) different parties in public services cannot effectively use resources in a mutually and socially responsible manner; (3) misaligned behaviours due to opportunism and lack of trust/information.

Additionally, within the PA literature, *public value destruction* research has been carried out. Bozeman (2002) was the first to note, in contrast to Moore's preoccupation with value creation, that it is possible public services/products fail to meet PV criteria (shown as reinforced inequalities, loss of democracy, etc.). A small number of subsequent studies further investigated the substance of PV destruction (Bozeman and Johnson 2015; Steen et al. 2018; Williams et al. 2016). Based on these prior studies, Cluley and Radnor (2020) called for more research into the 'disvalue' in public services, particularly regarding the situations where some citizen groups are excluded/rejected/sacrificed in some 'socially valuable' public projects, public resource are captured by individual groups, and PV is ill-defined.

Taken together, value destruction research offers a revolutionary way to understand the failures and problems in public services. Differentiated from market-failure or government-failure theories, value destruction theory maintains that public services should be judged upon their potential to facilitate value creation (Cui and Osborne 2023b). As a summary, Figure 4 conceptualizes value destruction in public services into a continuum, depending on different levels of severity. It offers a heuristic classification, while further research on different variations of value destruction is needed.

4.2.2 Value Destruction in the Complex Public Service Context

Subsection 4.2 depicted the broader context of public services where citizen participation takes place. Within this context, value destruction can equally happen. Based on studies reviewed, we conducted Figure 5 to explain three types of value destruction in different citizen participation stages, together with the fourth type of value destruction related to the broader conflicts in PSEs.

	Different types of value destruction	
Less severe		More severe
Value diminution	Value failure	Value deduction
The suboptimal value realization– a service can partially create some value for some groups of users and stakeholders (Vafeas et al., 2016).	*A service is failed to make changes. Value is failed to be created as expected (Skålén et al., 2015a).*	*A service fails to make positive changes, even diminishes pre-existed value, and makes service users' lives or our society worse (Cui & Osborne, 2022).*

Figure 4 A spectrum of value destruction according to the severity.

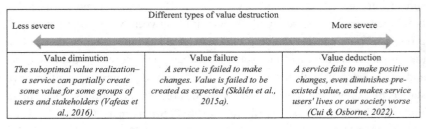

Figure 5 Value destruction in the PSE.

Value destruction in design/preparation: Citizens can participate in public services as co-designers by which creating value – showing as the development of personal skills and confidence. However, value destruction can occur when (1) citizens refuse to participate in co-design because they undervalue certain public services/projects (Cui and Osborne 2023a), and (2) some citizens are rejected from or misrepresented in the public service design process by the prevailing professional/political interests. Our vaccination research also revealed that citizen groups and communities were not widely included in the service design when the government needed to make fast decisions to prevent the spread of Covid-19.

Value destruction in service encounters: Value destruction can occur when citizens, as public service users, interact with providers. Reasons for this destruction can be mistakes, providers' incompetence and the interpersonal conflicts between providers and users (Engen et al. 2021). Power asymmetries can also make citizens dissatisfied, resentful and/or even behave disruptively (Flemig and Osborne 2019; Straussman 2022).

Value destruction in service use/consumption: When consuming the public service offerings independently, citizens can destroy value in their own lives, primarily due to the intentional or unintentional misuse of resources (Järvi et al. 2018). A typical example is the vaccine resistance and hesitancy, as well as the prevalence of anti-vaccine conspiracies during the Covid-19 vaccination project in Scotland. Furthermore, frustrations derived from prior interactions in the public service delivery process can also lead to maladaptive behaviour by public service users. This can ultimately limit or destroy their own value and/or exacerbate pre-existing individual and societal problems.

Value destruction associated with broader conflicts in the PSE: The PSE framework situates value creation in a multi-layer nested structure, comprising different stakeholders, as well as diversified societal institutions and individual values. These stakeholders usually have differentiated, rather than shared value expectations, regarding how a certain public service can help individuals and society. These value expectations may conflict with each other, resulting in one type of value created at the cost of another, or the destruction of both public and private value (Cui and Osborne 2023).

For instance, from our research on the Covid-19 vaccination project in Scotland, we found that the logistical requirement of speedy vaccine deployment has led to a government-centred, top-down service plan. This plan, however, set up obstacles for citizen participation in service design and delivery, which results in problems of inclusivity and justice (e.g., low vaccine coverage in rural Scotland and deprived communities). Another example is that vaccination policies for pregnant women were changed several times according to emerging medical evidence and statistical data. These changes may fulfil PVs like evidence-based and adaptive policy design, but they have exacerbated concerns in the general public and exacerbated vaccine hesitancy.

4.2.3 Implications for Theory and Practice

This section further expands our discussion on citizen participation by linking it with its ultimate outcome – value creation and/or destruction. It lays out the process of citizen participation, categorizes it into several stages, and elaborates on citizens' roles in creating value at each stage. Additionally, it elucidates the necessary institutions and technologies to facilitate participation and value creation. The second subsection unpacks the concept of value destruction, explaining its substance and occurrence within the PSE context.

Given that public services address multiple public and private value creation objectives, value destruction is an inherent element of public service delivery. Therefore, public managers and policymakers should not privilege either public or private value creation, but need to focus on the relationship between them. Figure 5 illustrates the value destruction throughout the entire public service process and within the complicated PSE context. Future research can test/ develop this framework in different empirical fields and further explore its theoretical and practical consequences.

5 Research Gaps and Implications for the Future: Integrating Theory and Practice for Value Creation in Service Delivery

This Element situates citizens' participation in public service delivery and its contribution to value creation. It presents the concept of citizens' engagement along the successive waves of public management reforms and its limited role despite noble intentions.

It positions participation at the core of the PSL, advocating for a strategic orientation to citizens' engagement in public service delivery processes. Subsequently, the Element summarizes the motives, incentives, and engagement tools to inform the institutional setting where participation may occur. Thus, it recognizes the need to frame appropriately the context of public services, accounting for the dynamic relationships and behaviours among the actors, institutions, and processes of public service. It argues that participation should be framed in the context of PSEs, where all the elements and actors of public services interact. As an alternative, it offers a more holistic framing of participation drawn upon PSL. At the core of this theory, intrinsic and extrinsic participation represents a necessary element of value creation (or destruction) for all public service stakeholders.

It develops a new approach to participation in the theory and practice of public services. Public services are essential for ensuring the well-being of citizens and promoting social development. However, our contribution is also the area of participation that research must explore to offer practice recommendations.

5.1 Conceptual Clarity

One of the primary challenges in researching citizens' participation and public services is the need for conceptual clarity. There needs to be a consensus on what constitutes participation, how it should be measured, and what value it produces. This Element starts by framing the concept around the different waves of public management reforms. Evidence from the traditional PA streams of the literature shows that citizen participation has yet to be integrated into decision-making structures and remains peripheral. The achievement of citizen participation is hindered by various factors, including the normative stance of some narratives, the dominance of a linear model of public service delivery, a focus on structural rather than processual change, and a failure to address power imbalances inherent in public services. We situate participation along the alternative model of PSL, which requires the appreciation of the intrinsic participation processes in delivering these services and the fundamental role of public service users and citizens during these processes. Under PSL, participation is a natural element of public service and requires a citizen's strategic orientation (Osborne et al. 2021). Therefore, it must be consciously engaged rather than allowing it to impact public service outcomes and value creation by default.

Subsequently, a pragmatic and sensitive approach to extrinsic forms of participation is necessary to link the application of co-production and co-design in public service delivery to the individual and societal context of the needs that these services address.

5.2 Framing the Space of Participation

Public Service Logic argues that public services should be explored and researched as services. The service lens provides the opportunity to appreciate the dynamics of public service delivery. This approach is underpinned by the centrality of 'co-production' and 'value'. The former recognizes the *intrinsic* and *active* role of the multiple actors, including citizens, that contribute to the public service processes, the latter emphasizes the 'value-added' to a service user by experiencing the service. Vargo and Lusch (2016) hence argue that value creation is not solely the purview of individual PSOs but occurs within complex and interactive relationships, comprising the key actors and processes of value creation as well as societal/institutional values and rules. To understand the complexity of participation in public service delivery and its role in value creation at the societal, service, and individual levels we suggest a new framing of the space to explore public service delivery: the PSE (Mustak and Plé 2020; Payne et al. 2021).

The PSE is a relational model where value originates through its elements' interconnected dynamics. Participation must be situated within this space to recognize the complex interdependencies between the various actors and stakeholders involved in delivering public services to ensure that public services are delivered in a meaningful and relevant way to the lives of citizens. By engaging the PSE actors more directly and effectively in the design, implementation, and evaluation of public services, services may be delivered in a way that is more effective, efficient, and responsive to the needs of citizens.

5.3 New Models of Participation in Public Services

Framing participation under the theory of PSL, adopting a PSE approach requires new models of participation in public services that recognize its intrinsic nature and the explicit contribution of a plurality of actors that move beyond the dyadic relationship PSO-citizen. Consequently, appropriate institutional arrangements must be explored to account for the interconnected relationships among the actors and their influence (Sorensen and Torfig 2021). For example, the literature on collaborative governance offers insights into the structures of decision-making processes. Participation is crucial to collaborative governance structures, enabling stakeholders to contribute their expertise, knowledge, and experiences to decision-making (Bianchi et al. 2021). New institutional arrangements of public service delivery based on PSL should explore how collaborative governance and participation address the complex dynamics among the elements of the PSE by bringing together diverse perspectives and expertise and reflecting the needs and values of the communities they serve for public service value.

More research is needed to identify adequate institutional arrangements for promoting citizen participation and to understand how these arrangements can be implemented in different contexts. The current literature on the motives of participation and the incentives to foster it must account for the PSE space.

The increasing availability of digital technologies has created new opportunities for participation in public services. However, more research is still needed on the use of technology to facilitate participation. Further research is needed to understand technology's potential benefits and challenges to enhance citizens' and other public service actors' participation in public services. Further research is needed to develop a clear and consistent conceptual framework for the participation of all the actors in the PSEs.

5.4 Participation and Value

Participation and value co-creation are concepts that have gained increasing attention in the public service sector in recent years. Participation refers to the involvement of citizens and other stakeholders in the design, delivery, and evaluation of public services. On the other hand, value co-creation refers to the process by which public services are designed and delivered in a dynamic relationship with citizens and other stakeholders to create value that meets their needs and expectations. In a traditional PAM setting, public service performance is often measured in terms of efficiency, effectiveness, and responsiveness to citizens' needs. In the traditional model of public service delivery, the government is responsible for designing and delivering services, and citizens are passive recipients of these services. However, this model needs to recognize the intrinsic and active role of citizens and other actors in the service processes and their contribution to value creation.

Under PSL, participation and value co-creation provides an alternative approach to public service delivery that seeks to overcome the limitations of the traditional model. Public service providers can better understand their needs and preferences and tailor services by engaging with citizens and other stakeholders in the design and delivery of services. This may lead to more efficient and effective service delivery and higher citizen satisfaction and engagement levels.

The differences between public service performance in the traditional and participatory models can be seen in various areas. For example, the traditional PAM models focus on delivering services efficiently and effectively, with little consideration given to citizens' preferences or involvement. In contrast, the PSL model focuses on co-creating value with citizens and other stakeholders, intending to deliver services that meet their needs and expectations. How participation contributes to value creation still needs to be investigated. Although some evidence suggests that citizen participation can improve service quality, rigorous empirical studies in this area still need to be conducted. More research is needed to understand the mechanisms by which participation can lead to value creation and identify the conditions under which it is most effective.

Regarding accountability, the traditional model places the responsibility for service delivery solely on the government, whereas the participatory model involves citizens and other stakeholders monitoring and evaluating service performance. However, more research still needs to be done on the long-term sustainability of citizen participation initiatives. More research is needed to understand the factors contributing to the sustainability of citizen participation initiatives and identify strategies for promoting their long-term viability. Integrating theory for value creation in public service delivery is critical to the success of PSOs in the future. The research agenda for the future should focus on developing new metrics for measuring the value created in public service delivery, developing new service delivery models that leverage technology and innovation, optimizing existing service delivery models, and exploring the impact of social and economic factors on public service delivery and value creation.

Participation under PSL in a PSE comes at a cost. It is a more challenging and contentious approach, but it is essential to be governed to evolve public service theory and advocate for public service value creation.

Indeed, the evolving context surrounding public service delivery, influenced by various factors such as technological, demographic, geopolitical, and societal changes, may significantly impact the values inherent in co-production under PSL and affect value. Given the evolving landscape shaped by technological advancements, demographic shifts, geopolitical transformations, and changing tastes and behaviours of citizens, the context in which public services are delivered undergoes continuous flux, impacting the values associated with these services. And potentially the value created or destroyed in public service provision. Technological changes, such as advancements in artificial intelligence and digitalization, alter the way services are accessed and experienced, prompting shifts in societal expectations and preferences. Demographic changes, including aging populations and urbanization, influence the demand for specific services and redefine notions of inclusivity and accessibility. Geopolitical changes, such as shifts in governance structures or international relations, can reshape the priorities and funding allocations for public services. Moreover, changes in citizens' tastes and behaviours, driven by cultural shifts and socio-economic factors, demand responsiveness and adaptability from public service providers. Understanding and navigating these multifaceted changes are essential for public service organizations to effectively address emerging needs within their respective contexts that may shape the *value in context*.

As these contextual dynamics shift, they may redefine the nature and scope of co-production efforts and subsequently affect value creation at both the individual and societal levels. This nuanced interplay between changing contexts and co-production practices represents a crucial domain for investigation, one that warrants further attention beyond the scope of the current manuscript. Exploring how shifting values in context influence the mechanisms and outcomes of co-production under PSL can offer valuable insights into enhancing the effectiveness and responsiveness of public service delivery. By acknowledging and addressing this gap in research, future studies can contribute to a deeper understanding of the complex dynamics shaping contemporary public service provision and value creation.

Conclusion

In conclusion, this Element has provided a comprehensive examination of citizens' participation in public service delivery and its role in value creation. Tracing the evolution of participation across various waves of public management reforms has highlighted the limited integration of participation into decision-making structures despite its noble intentions. Emphasizing participation as a core element of PSL, this Element advocates for a strategic approach to citizens' engagement, recognizing its intrinsic value in service delivery processes. It has underscored the importance of framing participation within the dynamic context of PSEs, acknowledging the complex interdependencies among actors, institutions, and processes. However, as the context of public service delivery continues to evolve and is influenced by technological, demographic, geopolitical, and societal changes, there remains a need to explore how these shifting values affect co-production efforts and value creation. This represents a critical research gap that warrants further investigation to enhance our understanding of contemporary public service provision and value creation in an ever-changing landscape. By integrating theory and practice, future research endeavours can contribute to the advancement of public service delivery models that are more responsive, efficient, and effective in meeting the evolving needs of citizens and society.

References

Agranoff, R., & McGuire, M. (2003). Collaborative Public Management: New Strategies for Local Governments. Washington, DC: Georgetown University Press.

Akaka, M. A., & Schau, H. J. (2019). Value creation in consumption journeys: Recursive reflexivity and practice continuity. Journal of the Academy of Marketing Science, 47, 499–515.

Alford, J. (2002). Why do public-sector clients coproduce? Toward a contingency theory. Administration & Society, 34(1), 32–56.

Alford, J. (2009). Engaging public sector clients: From service-delivery to co-production. Basingstoke: Palgrave-Macmillan.

Alford, J. (2016). Co-production, interdependence and publicness: Extending public service-dominant logic. Public Management Review, 18(5), 673–691.

Alford, J., & O'Flynn, J. (2009). Making sense of Public Value: Concepts, critiques and emergent meanings. International Journal of Public Administration, 32, 171–191.

Amabile, T. M. (1993). Motivational synergy: Toward new conceptualizations of intrinsic and extrinsic motivation in the workplace. Human Resource Management Review, 3(3), 185–201.

Amabile, T. M., Hill, K. G., Hennessey, B. A., & Tighe, E. M. (1994). The work preference inventory: Assessing intrinsic and extrinsic motivational orientations. Journal of Personality and Social Psychology, 66(5), 950–967.

Ampatzidou, C., Constantinescu, T., Berger, M., et al. (2018). All work and no play? Facilitating serious games and gamified applications in participatory urban planning and governance. Urban Planning, 3(1), 34–46.

An, S. H., & Meier, K. J. (2022). Optimal turnover rates and performance in public organizations: Theoretical expectations. Public Performance & Management Review, 45(3), 582–604.

Andersen, S. C., Jakobsen, M., Serritzlew, S., & Thomsen, M. K. (2017). Coproduction of public services. In O. James, S. R. Jilke, & G. G. Van Ryzin (Eds.), Experiments in Public Management Research: Challenges and Contributions (pp. 329–344). Cambridge University Press.

Arienzo, M. M., Collins, M., & Jennings, K. S. (2021). Enhancing engagement of citizen scientists to monitor precipitation phase. Frontiers in Earth Science, 9, 68.

Arnkil, R., Järvensivu, A., Koski, P., & Piirainen, T. (2010). Exploring quadruple helix outlining user-oriented innovation models. University of Tampere,

Institute for Social Research Työraportteja 85/2010 Working Papers. https:// trepo.tuni.fi/bitstream/handle/10024/65758/978-951-44-8209-0.pdf

Asingizwe, D., Poortvliet, P. M., Koenraadt, C. J., et al. (2020). Why (not) participate in citizen science? Motivational factors and barriers to participate in a citizen science program for malaria control in Rwanda. PLoS One, 15(8), e0237396.

August, T. A., West, S. E., Robson, H., et al. (2019). Citizen meets social science: Predicting volunteer involvement in a global freshwater monitoring experiment. Freshwater Science, 38(2), 321–331.

Bellandi, M., Donati, L., & Cataneo, A. (2021). Social innovation governance and the role of universities: Cases of quadruple helix partnerships in Italy. Technological Forecasting and Social Change, 164, 120518.

Bellé, N. (2015). Performance-related pay and the crowding out of motivation in the public sector: A randomized field experiment. Public Administration Review, 75(2), 230–241.

Benington, J. (2011). From private choice to public value. In J. Benington, & M. Moore (Eds.), Public Value: Theory and Practice (pp. 31–49). Basingstoke: Palgrave-Macmillan.

Bianchi, C., Nasi, G., & Rivenbark, W. C. (2021). Implementing collaborative governance: Models, experiences, and challenges. Public Management Review, 23(11), 1581–1589.

Blau, M. (1964). Exchange and Power in Social Life. New York: John Wiley.

Borghys, K., Van Der Graaf, S., Walravens, N., & Van Compernolle, M. (2020). Multi-stakeholder innovation in smart city discourse: Quadruple helix thinking in the age of 'platforms'. Frontiers in Sustainable Cities, 2, 5.

Bovaird, T. (2007). Beyond engagement and participation – user and community co-production of public service. Public Administration Review, 67, 846–860.

Bovaird, T., & Loeffler, E. (2012). From engagement to co-production: The contribution of users and communities to outcomes and public value. Voluntas: International Journal of Voluntary and Nonprofit Organizations, 23 (4), 1119–1138.

Bovaird, T., Stoker, G., Jones, T., Loeffler, E., & Pinilla Roncancio, M. (2016). Promouvoir la coproduction collective des services publics: Comment encourager les citoyens à participer à des mécanismes de gouvernance complexes au Royaume-Uni. Revue Internationale des Sciences Administratives, 82, 53–75.

Bozeman, B. (2002). Public-value failure: When efficient markets may not do. Public Administration Review, 62(2), 145–161.

Bozeman, B. (2007). Public values and public interest: Counterbalancing economic individualism. Washington, DC: Georgetown University Press.

Bozeman, B., & Johnson, J. (2015). The political economy of public values: A case for the public sphere and progressive opportunity. The American Review of Public Administration, 45(1), 61–85.

Brandsen, T., & Helderman, J. K. (2012). The conditions for successful co-production in housing: A case study of German housing cooperatives. In V. Pestoff, T. Brandsen, & B. Verschuere (Eds.), New Public Governance, the Third Sector and Co-production (pp. 169–191). London: Routledge.

Brandsen, T., & Honingh, M. (2016). Distinguishing different types of coproduction: A conceptual analysis based on the classical definitions. Public Administration Review, 76(3), 427–435.

Brewer, G. A., & Selden, S. C. (2000). Why elephants gallop: Assessing and predicting organizational performance in federal agencies. Journal of Public Administration Research and Theory, 10(4), 685–712.

Brief, A. P., & Aldag, R. J. (1977). The intrinsic-extrinsic dichotomy: Toward conceptual clarity. Academy of Management Review, 2(3), 496–500.

Bright, L. F., & Margetts, H. (2018). The promise and pitfalls of digital-enabled participation: A review of the literature. Policy & Internet, 10(3), 309–338.

Brodie, R., Ranjan, K., Verreynne, M.-l., Jiang, Y., & Previte, J. (2021). Coronavirus crisis and health care: Learning from a service ecosystem perspective. Journal of Service Theory and Practice, 31(2), 225–246.

Brudney, J., & England, R. (1983). Toward a definition of the co-production concept. Public Administration Review, 43(1), 59–65.

Brugue, Q., & Gallego, R. (2003). A democratic public administration? Developments in public participation and innovations in community governance. Public Management Review, 5(3), 425–447.

Bryson, J., Sancino, A., Benington, J., & Sørensen, E. (2017). Towards a multi-actor theory of public value co-creation. Public Management Review, 19(5), 640–654.

Bryson, J. M., Crosby, B. C., & Bloomberg, L. (2014). Public value governance: Moving beyond traditional public administration and the new public management. Public Administration Review, 74(4), 445–456.

Burby, R. J. (2003). Making plans that matter: Citizen involvement and government action. Journal of the American Planning Association, 69(1), 33–49.

Chang, W., & Taylor, S. A. (2016). The effectiveness of customer participation in new product development: A meta-analysis. Journal of Marketing, 80(1), 47–64.

Christensen, T., & Laegreid, P. (2011). Democracy and administrative policy: Contrasting elements of New Public Management and post-NPM. European Policy Science Review, 3(1), 125–146.

Ciasullo, M., Troisi, O., & Leone, D. (2020). Multi-level governance for sustainable innovation in smart communities: An ecosystems approach. International Entrepreneurship and Management Journal, (16), 1167–1195.

Clark, P., & Wilson, J. (1961). Incentive systems: A theory of organisations. Administrative Science Quarterly, 6, 129–166.

Clarke, A., & Craft, J. (2018). The twin faces of public sector design. Governance, 32(1), 5–21.

Cluley, V., & Radnor, Z. (2020). Progressing the conceptualization of value co-creation in public service organizations. Perspectives on Public Management and Governance, 3(3), 211–221.

Commission on the Future Delivery of Public Services (2011). Report of the Commission on the Future Delivery of Public Services. Scotland: Scottish Government.

Compagnucci, L., Spigarelli, F., Coelho, J., & Duarte, C. (2021). Living Labs and user engagement for innovation and sustainability. Journal of Cleaner Production, 289, 125721.

Cooper, M. H., & Culyer, T. (1968). The Price of Blood. London: Institute of Economic Affairs.

Cordella, A., & Paletti, A. (2019). ICTs and value creation in public sector: Manufacturing logic vs service logic. Information Polity, 23(2), 125–141.

Cui, T., & Osborne, S. P. (2023a). Unpacking value destruction at the intersection between public and private value. Public Administration, 101(4), 1207–1226.

Cui, T., & Osborne, S. P. (2023b). New development: Value destruction in public service delivery – a process model and its implications. Public Money & Management, 43(2), 187–190.

Dahl, A., & Soss, J. (2014). Neoliberalism for the common good? Public value governance and the downsizing of democracy. Public Administration Review, July/August, 74(4), 496–504.

Deci, E. L., & Ryan, R. M. (2010). Self-determination. In I. B. Weiner, & W. E. Craighead (Eds.), The Corsini Encyclopedia of Psychology (1–2).

deLeon, L., & Denhardt, R. B. (2000). The political theory of reinvention. Public Administration Review, 60(2), 89–97.

Denhardt, J. V., & Denhardt, R. B. (2015). New Public Service: Serving, Not Steering. New York: Routledge.

Denhardt, R. B., & Denhardt, J. V. (2000). The New Public Service: Serving Rather than Steering. Public Administration Review, 60(6), 549–559.

Deshpande, R., Farley, J., & Webster, F. (1993). Corporate culture customer orientation and innovativeness in Japanese firms: A quadrad analysis. Journal of Marketing, 57(1), 23–37.

Dickinson, J. L., Shirk, J., Bonter, D., et al. (2012). The current state of citizen science as a tool for ecological research and public engagement. Frontiers in Ecology and the Environment, 10(6), 291–297.

Dietrich, T., Trischler, J., Schuster, L., & Rundle-Thiele, S. (2017). Co-designing services with vulnerable consumers. Journal of Service Theory and Practice, 27(3), 663–688.

Dudau, A., Glennon, R., & Verschuere, B. (2019). Following the yellow brick road?(Dis) enchantment with co-design, co-production and value co-creation in public services. Public Management Review, 21(11), 1577–1594.

Echeverri, P., & Skålén, P. (2011). Co-creation and co-destruction: A practice-theory based study of interactive value formation. Marketing Theory, 11(3), 351–373.

Echeverri, P., & Skålén, P. (2021). Value co-destruction: Review and conceptualization of interactive value formation. Marketing Theory, 21(2), 227–249.

Egger-Peitler, I., Hammerschmid, G., & Meyer, R. (2007). Motivation, Identification, and Incentive Preferences as Issues for Modernization and HR Strategies in Local Government? First Evidence from Austria. Paper presented at the Annual Conference of the European Group of Public Administration, Madrid, Spain, September 19–22.

Emerson, K., Nabatchi, T., & Balogh, S. (2012). An integrative framework for collaborative governance. Journal of Public Administration Research and Theory, 22(1), 1–29.

Engen, M., Fransson, M., Quist, J., & Skålén, P. (2021). Continuing the development of the public service logic: A study of value co-destruction in public services. Public Management Review, 23, 886–905.

Espersson, M., & Westrup, U. (2020). Value destruction in Swedish welfare services: Frontline workers' impact on asylumseeking minors' possibilities of creating value in early integration. International Journal of Public Administration, 43(2), 115–125.

Farr, M. (2018). Power dynamics and collaborative mechanisms in co-production and co-design processes. Critical Social Policy, 38(4), 623–644.

Fellnhofer, K. (2017). Facilitating entrepreneurial discovery in smart specialisation via stakeholder participation within online mechanisms for knowledge-based policy advice. Cogent Business & Management, 4(1), 1296802.

Fischer, F. (2006). Participatory governance as deliberative empowerment: The cultural politics of discursive space. The American Review of Public Administration, 36(1), 19–40.

Flemig, S., & Osborne, S. (2019). The dynamics of co-production in the context of social care personalization. Journal of Social Policy, 48(4), 671–697.

Flinders, M., Wood, M., & Cunningham, M. (2016). The politics of co-production: Risks, limits and pollution. Evidence & Policy, 12(2), 261–279.

Frederickson, H. G. (1980). The New Public Administration. Tuscaloosa: University of Alabama Press.

Fuster Morell, M., & Senabre Hidalgo, E. (2022). Co-creation applied to public policy: A case study on collaborative policies for the platform economy in the city of Barcelona. CoDesign, 18(3), 378–397.

Gagné, M., & Deci, E. L. (2005). Self-determination theory and work motivation. Journal of Organizational Behavior, 26, 331–362.

Gebauer, H., Johnson, M., & Enquist, B. (2010). Value co-creation as a determinant of success in public transport services: A study of the Swiss Federal Railway operator (SBB). Managing Service Quality: An International Journal, 20(6), 511–530.

Gofen, A. (2015). Citizens' entrepreneurial role in public service provision. Public Management Review, 17(3), 404–424.

Golumbic, Y. N., Baram-Tsabari, A., & Koichu, B. (2019). Engagement and communication features of scientifically successful citizen science projects. Environmental Communication, 14(4), 465–480.

Grant, A. M. (2008). Does intrinsic motivation fuel the prosocial fire? Motivational synergy in predicting persistence, performance, and productivity. Journal of Applied Psychology, 93(1), 48.

Greenaway, J., Salter, B., & Hart, S. (2007). How policy networks can damage democratic health: A case study in the government of governance. Public Administration, 85(3), 717–738.

Grönroos, C. (2017). On value and value creation in service: A management perspective. Journal of Creating Value, 3(2), 125–141.

Grönroos, C. (2019). Reforming public services: Does service logic have anything to offer? Public Management Review, 21(5), 775–788.

Grönroos, C., & Voima, P. (2013). Critical service logic: Making sense of value creation and co-creation. Journal of the Academy of Marketing Science, 41(2), 133–150.

Hardyman, W., Kitchener, M., & Daunt, K. L. (2019). What matters for me! User conceptions of value in specialist cancer care. Public Management Review, 21(11), 1687–1706.

Hodgkinson, I., Hannibal, C., Keating, B., Chester-Buxton, R., & Bateman, N. (2017). Towards a public service management. Journal of Service Management, 28(5), 998–1023.

Hood, C. (1991). A public management for all seasons? Public Administration, 63, 3–19.

Hood, C., Dunsire, A., & Thomson, L. (1988). Rolling back the state: Thatcherism, fraserism and bureaucracy. Governance, 1(3), 243–270.

Horner, L., & Hutton, W. (2011). Public value, deliberative democracy and the role of public managers. In J. Benington, & M. Moore (Eds.), Public Value: Theory and Practice (pp. 1–53). Basingstoke: Palgrave-Macmillan.

Ingraham, P., & Rosenbloom, D. H. (1989). The new public personnel and the new public service. Public Administration Review, 49(2), 115–126.

Jackson, C. B., Østerlund, C., Crowston, K., Harandi, M., & Trouille, L. (2020). Shifting forms of engagement: Volunteer learning in online citizen science. Proceedings of the ACM on Human-Computer Interaction, 4(CSCW1), 1–19.

Jakobsen, M. (2013). Can government initiatives increase citizen coproduction? Results of a randomized field experiment. Journal of Public Administration Research and Theory, 23(1), 27–54.

Jakobsen, M., & Andersen, S. C. (2013). Coproduction and equity in public service delivery. Public Administration Review, 73(5), 704–713.

Järvi, H., Kähkönen, A. K., & Torvinen, H. (2018). When value co-creation fails: Reasons that lead to value co-destruction. Scandinavian Journal of Management, 34(1), 63–77.

Jennett, C., Kloetzer, L., Schneider, D., et al. (2016). Motivations, learning and creativity in online citizen science. Journal of Science Communication, 15(3), 1–23.

Jilke, S., & Van Ryzin, G. G. (2020). Crowdsourcing and the public sector: A review and research agenda. Public Management Review, 22(7), 1023–1041.

Jun, K. N., & Bryer, T. (2017). Facilitating public participation in local governments in hard times. American Review of Public Administration, 47(7), 840–856.

Karp, T., & Helg, T. (2008). From change management to change leadership: Embracing chaotic change in public service organizations. Journal of Change Management, 8(1), 85–96.

Kennedy, A., Cosgrave, C., Macdonald, J., et al. (2021). Translating co-design from face-to-face to online: An Australian primary producer project conducted during COVID-19. International Journal of Environmental Research and Public Health, 18(8), 41–47.

Kimbell, L. (2011). Designing for service as one way of designing services. International Journal of Design, 5(2), 41–52.

Kinder, T., Six, F., Stenvall, J., & Memon, A. (2022). Governance-as-legitimacy: Are ecosystems replacing networks? Public Management Review, 24(1), 8–33.

Kinder, T., Stenvall, J., Six, F., & Memon, A. (2021). Relational leadership in collaborative governance ecosystems. Public Management Review, 23(11), 1612–1639.

Kleinhans, R. (2017). False promises of co-production in neighbourhood regeneration: The case of Dutch community enterprises. Public Management Review, 19(10), 1500–1518.

Knapp, M. (1984). Economics of Social Care. London: Macmillan.

Kragh, G. (2016). The motivations of volunteers in citizen science. Environmental Scientist, 25(2), 32–35.

Laamanen, M., & Skålén, P. (2015). Collective – conflictual value co-creation: A strategic action field approach. Marketing Theory, 15(3), 381–400.

Lakomý, M., Hlavová, R., Machackova, H., et al. (2020). The motivation for citizens' involvement in life sciences research is predicted by age and gender. PLoS One, 15(8), e0237140.

LaPorte, T. (1971). The recovery of relevance in the study of public administration. In F. Marini (Ed.), Toward a New Public Administration: The Minnowbrook Perspective (pp. 17–48). Scranton: Chandler.

Larson, L. R., Cooper, C. B., Futch, S., et al. (2020). The diverse motivations of citizen scientists: Does conservation emphasis grow as volunteer participation progresses? Biological Conservation, 242, 108428.

Laud, G., Bove, L., Ranaweera, C., et al. (2019). Value co-destruction: A typology of resource mis-integration manifestations. Journal of Services Marketing, 33(7), 866–889.

Leite, H., & Hodgkinson, I. (2021). Examining resilience across a service ecosystem under crisis. Public Management Review, 25(4), 690–709.

Lember, V., Brandsen, T., & Tõnurist, P. (2019). The potential impacts of digital technologies on co-production and co-creation. Public Management Review, 21(11), 1665–1686.

Loeffler, E., & Bovaird, T. (2016). User and community co-production of public services: What does the evidence tell us? International Journal of Public Administration, 39(13), 1006–1019.

Lowndes, V., Pratchett, L., & Stoker, G. (2001). Trends in public participation: Part I – local government perspectives. Public Administration, 79(1), 205–222.

McLaughlin, K., Osborne, S., & Chew, C. (2009). Relationship marketing, relational capital and the future of marketing in public service organizations. Public Money and Management, 29(1), 35–42.

Mediano, J., & Ruiz-Alba, J. (2019). Customer orientation in highly relational services. Marketing Intelligence & Planning. https://doi.org/10.1108/MIP-02-2019-0127.

Meijer, A. J., & Thaens, M. (2018). Digital social innovation for public services: Co-creating change by empowering citizens. Government Information Quarterly, 35(4), 567–573.

Mergel, I., Bellé, N., & Nasi, G. (2021). Prosocial motivation of private sector IT professionals joining government. Review of Public Personnel Administration, 41(2), 338–357.

Meynhardt, T., & Jasinenko, A. (2020). Measuring public value: Scale development and construct validation. International Public Management Journal, 24(2), 222–249.

Miller, G. J., & Whitford, A. B. (2007). The principal's moral hazard: Constraints on the use of incentives in hierarchy. Journal of Public Administration Research and Theory, 17, 213–233.

Millward, L. (2005). Just because we are amateurs doesn't mean we aren't professional: The importance of expert activists in tenant participation. Public Administration, 83(3), 735–751.

Moore, M., & Benington, J. (2011). Conclusions: Looking ahead. In J. Benington, & M. Moore (Eds.), Public Value: Theory and Practice (256–274). Basingstoke: Palgrave-Macmillan.

Moore, M. H. (1995). Creating Public Value: Strategic Management in Government. Cambridge, MA: Harvard University Press.

Moseley, A., James, O., John, P., et al. (2018). The effects of social information on volunteering: A field experiment. Nonprofit and Voluntary Sector Quarterly, 47(3), 583–603.

Musso, J. A., Young, M. M., & Thom, M. (2019). Volunteerism as co-production in public service management: Application to public safety in California. Public Management Review, 21(4), 473–494.

Mustak, M., & Plé, L. (2020). A critical analysis of service ecosystems research: Rethinking its premises to move forward. Journal of Services Marketing, 34(3), 399–413.

Nabatchi, T. (2018). Public values frames in administration and governance. Perspectives on Public Management and Governance, 1(1), 59–72.

Nabatchi, T., & Leighninger, M. (2015). Public Participation for 21st Century Democracy. Hoboken, NJ: John Wiley & Sons.

Nabatchi, T., Sancino, A., & Sicilia, M. (2017). Varieties of participation in public services: The who, when, and what of coproduction. Public Administration Review, 77(5), 766–776.

Nasi, G., & Choi, H. (2023). Design strategies for Citizen Strategic Orientation. Public Management Review, 1–20. https://doi.org/10.1080/14719037.2023.2228316

Novaro, R., Nasi, G., Angelou, M., & Stylianidis, E. (2021). Manual for Citizen Science Community Building. Incentive. https://incentive-project.eu/wp-content/uploads/2022/04/INCENTIVE-D2.3_Manual-for-Citizen-Science-Community-Building-final.pdf.

O'Flynn, J. (2007). From new public management to public value: Framework change and managerial implications. The Australian Journal of Public Administration, 66(3), 353–366.

O'Flynn, J. (2021). Where to for public value? Taking stock and moving on. International Journal of Public Administration, 44(10), 867–877. https://doi.org/10.1080/01900692.2021.1884696.

OECD (2017). Engaging citizens in co-creation in public services. OECD Public Governance Reviews. Paris: OECD.

Oksman, V., & Kulju, M. (2017). Developing online illustrative and participatory tools for urban planning: Towards open innovation and co-production through citizen engagement. International Journal of Services Technology and Management, 23(5–6), 445–464.

Osborne, S. (2010). The New Public Governance? London: Routledge.

Osborne, S. (2021). Public Service Logic. London: Routledge.

Osborne, S., & Strokosch, K. (2022). Participation: Add-on or core component of public service delivery? Australian Journal of Public Administration, 81(1), 181–200.

Osborne, S., Cucciniello, M., Strokosch, K., & Nasi, G. (2020). Strategic user orientation in public services delivery – the missing link in the strategic trinity? Public Money & Management, 41(2), 172–175.

Osborne, S., Nasi, G., & Powell, M. (2021). Beyond co-production: Value co-creation in public services. Public Administration, 99(4), 641–657.

Osborne, S., Powell, M., Cui, T., & Strokosch, K. (2022). Value creation in the public service ecosystem: An integrative framework. Public Administration Review, 82(4), 634–645.

Osborne, S., Cucciniello, M., & Cui, T. (2024). Understanding vaccination programme through the lens of 'Public Service Logic': Towards a service ecosystem framework. Handbook on Public Management and COVID-19, (in-print).

Osborne, S. P. (2006). The new public governance? Public Management Review, 8(3), 377–387.

Osborne, S. P. (2020). Public Service Logic: Creating Value for Public Service Users, Citizens, and Society through Public Service Delivery. Oxfordshire, England, UK: Routledge.

Osborne, S. P., & Brown, L. (2011a). Innovation in public services: Engaging with risk. Public Money & Management, 31(1), 4–6.

Osborne, S. P., & Brown, L. (2011b). Innovation, public policy and public services delivery in the UK. The word that would be king? Public Administration, 89, 1335–1350.

Osborne, S. P., & Strokosch, K. (2013). It takes two to tango? British Journal of Management, 24, S31–S47.

Osborne, S. P., Nasi, G., & Radnor, Z. (2013). The service-dominant context of public services: A suitable case for treatment? In Context in Public Policy and Management (pp. 178–191). Edward Elgar Publishing.

Osborne, S. P., Radnor, Z., & Strokosch, K. (2016). Co-production and the co-creation of value in public services: A suitable case for treatment? Public Management Review, 18(5), 639–653.

Osborne, S., Powell, M., & Nasi, G. (2021). Beyond co-production: Value co-creation in public services. Public Administration, 99(4), 641–657.

Osborne, S. P., Nasi, G., & Powell, M. (2021). Beyond co-production: Value creation and public services. Public Administration, 99(4), 641–657.

Osborne, S. P., Cucciniello, M., Nasi, G., & Strokosch, K. (2021). New development: Strategic user orientation in public services delivery – the missing link in the strategic trinity? Public Money & Management, 41(2), 172–175.

Osborne, S. P., Powell, M., Cui, T., & Strokosch, K. (2022). Value creation in the public service ecosystem: An integrative framework. Public Administration Review, 82(4), 634–645.

Ostrom, E. (1996). Crossing the great divide: Coproduction, synergy, and development. World Development, 24(6), 1073–1087.

Payne, E. H., Dahl, A. J., & Peltier, J. (2021). Digital servitization value co-creation framework for AI services: A research agenda for digital transformation in financial service ecosystems. Journal of Research in Interactive Marketing, 15(2), 200–222.

Percy, S. (1984). Citizen participation in the co-production of urban services. Urban Affairs Quarterly, 19(4), 431–446.

Perry, J. L., Engbers, T. A., & Jun, S. Y. (2009). Back to the future? Performance-related pay, empirical research, and the perils of persistence. Public Administration Review, 69(1), 39–51.

Pestoff, V. (2006). Citizens and co-production of welfare services: Childcare in eight European countries. Public Management Review, 8(4), 503–519.

Pestoff, V. (2012a). Co-production and third sector social services in Europe: Some concepts and evidence. Voluntas: International Journal of Voluntary and Nonprofit Organizations, 23(4), 1102–1118.

Pestoff, V. (2012b). New Public Governance, co-production and third sector social services in Europe: Crowding in and crowding out. In V. Pestoff, T. Brandsen, & B. Verschuere (Eds.), New Public Governance, the Third Sector and Co-production (pp. 361–380). New York: Routledge.

Petrescu, M. (2019). From marketing to public value: Towards a theory of public service ecosystems. Public Management Review, 21(11), 1733–1752.

Petrovsky, N., Mok, J. Y., & León-Cázares, F. (2017). Citizen expectations and satisfaction in a young democracy: A test of the expectancy-disconfirmation model. Public Administration Review, 77(3), 395–407.

Plé, L., & Chumpitaz Cáceres, R. (2010). Not always co-creation: Introducing interactional co-destruction of value in service-dominant logic. Journal of Services Marketing, 24(6), 430–437.

Pollitt, C. (2013). Context in Public Policy and Management. Cheltenham: Elgar.

Pollitt, C., & Bouckaert, G. (2017). Public Management Reform: A Comparative Analysis. Oxford: Oxford University Press.

Porter, D. O. (2012). Co-production and network structures in public education. In V. Pestoff, T. Brandsen, & B. Verschuere (Eds.), New Public Governance, the Third Sector, and Co-production (145–168). New York: Routledge.

Porumbescu, G., Bellé, N., Cucciniello, M., & Nasi, G. (2017). Translating policy transparency into policy understanding and policy support: Evidence from a survey experiment. Public Administration, 95(4), 990–1008.

Porumbescu, G. A., Lindeman, M. I. H., Ceka, E., & Cucciniello, M. (2017). Can transparency foster more understanding and compliant citizens? Public Administration Review, 77, 840–850.

Powell, M., & Osborne, S. (2020). Social enterprises, marketing, and sustainable public service provision. International Review of Administrative Sciences, 86(1), 62–79. https://doi.org/10.1177/0020852317751244.

Powell, M., Greener, I., Szmigin, I., Doheny, S., & Mills, N. (2010). Broadening the focus of public service consumerism. Public Management Review, 12(3), 323–339.

Powell, M., Gillett, A., & Doherty, B. (2019). Sustainability in social enterprise: Hybrid organizing in public services. Public Management Review, 21(2), 159–186.

Prahalad, C. K., & Ramaswamy, V. (2004). The Future of Competition: Co-creating Unique Value with Customers. Brighton, Massachusetts: Harvard Business Press.

Putnam, R. D. (2000). Bowling Alone: The Collapse and Revival of American Community. New York, USA: Simon and Schuster.

Radnor, Z., Osborne, S., & Glennon, R. (2016). Public management theory. In Handbook on Theories of Governance (pp. 46–60). Cheltenham, UK: Edward Elgar. Edited by Christopher Ansell, Professor of Political Science, University of California, Berkeley, US and Jacob Torfing, Professor of Politics and Institutions, Department of Social Sciences and Business, Roskilde University, Denmark and Professor, Faculty of Social Sciences, Nord University, Norway.

Ritz, A., Brewer, G. A., & Neumann, O. (2016). Public service motivation: A systematic literature review and outlook. Public Administration Review, 76(3), 414–426.

Roberts, N. (2004). Public deliberation in an age of direct citizen participation. American Review of Public Administration, 34(4), 315–353.

Røhnebæk, M. T., François, V., Kiss, N., et al. (2024). Public service logic and the creation of value propositions through framing. Public Management Review, 26(2), 399–420.

Roman, M., Varga, H., Cvijanovic, V., & Reid, A. (2020). Quadruple Helix models for sustainable regional innovation: Engaging and facilitating civil society participation. Economies, 8(2), 48.

Rose, J., Flak, L. S., & Sæbø, Ø. (2018). Stakeholder theory for the E-government context: Framing a value-oriented normative core. Government Information Quarterly, 35(3), 362–374.

Rossi, P., & Tuurnas, S. (2021). Conflicts fostering understanding of value co-creation and service systems transformation in complex public service systems. Public Management Review, 23(2), 254–275.

Rotman, D., Preece, J., Hammock, J., et al. (2012, February). Dynamic changes in motivation in collaborative citizen-science projects. In Proceedings of the ACM 2012 Conference on Computer Supported Cooperative Work (pp. 217–226).

Rotman, D., Hammock, J., Preece, J. J., et al. (2014a, February). Does motivation in citizen science change with time and culture? In Proceedings of the Companion Publication of the 17th ACM Conference on Computer Supported Cooperative Work & Social Computing (pp. 229–232).

Rotman, D., Hammock, J., Preece, J., et al. (2014b). Motivations affecting initial and long-term participation in citizen science projects in three countries. IConference 2014 Proceedings.

Sanders, E. B., & Stappers, P. J. (2008). Co-Creation and the new landscapes of design. Co-Design, 4(1), 5–18.

Satorras, M., Ruiz-Mallén, I., Monterde, A., & March, H. (2020). Co-production of urban climate planning: Insights from the Barcelona Climate Plan. Cities, 106, 102887.

Schön, D. (1987). The Reflective Practitioner: How Professionals Think in Action. New York: Basic Books.

Schütz, F., Heidingsfelder, M. L., & Schraudner, M. (2019). Co-shaping the future in quadruple helix innovation systems: Uncovering public preferences toward participatory research and innovation. She Ji: The Journal of Design, Economics, and Innovation, 5(2), 128–146.

Scottish Government (2019). The Scottish Approach to Service Design. Edinburgh: Scottish Government.

Selada, C. (2017). Smart cities and the quadruple helix innovation systems conceptual framework: The case of Portugal. In The Quadruple Innovation Helix Nexus A Smart Growth Model, Quantitative Empirical Validation and Operationalization for OECD Countries Editors: Sara Paulina De Oliveira Monteiro, Elias G. Carayannis Publisher: Palgrave Macmillan US 2017.

Skålén, P., Pace, S., & Cova, B. (2015a). Firm-brand community value co-creation as alignment of practices. European Journal of Marketing, 49(3/4), 596–620.

Skålén, P., Aal, K. A., & Edvardsson, B. (2015b). Cocreating the Arab spring: Understanding transformation of service systems in contention. Journal of Service Research, 18(3), 250–264.

Skålén, P., Karlsson, J., Engen, M., & Magnuson, P. R. (2018). Understanding public service innovation as resource integration and creation of value propositions. Australian Journal of Public Administration, 77(4), 700–714.

Skarli, J. B. (2021). Creating or destructing value in use? Handling cognitive impairments in co-creation with serious and chronically ill users. Administrative Sciences, 11(1), 16.

Sørensen, E., & Torfing, J. (2011). Enhancing collaborative innovation in the public sector. Administration & Society, 43(8), 842–868.

Sorensen, E., & Torfing, J. (2018). The democratizing impact of governance networks: From pluralisation, via democratic anchorage, to interactive political leadership. Public Administration, 96(2), 302–317.

Sørensen, E., & Torfing, J. (2021). Radical and disruptive answers to downstream problems in collaborative governance? Public Management Review, 23(11), 1590–1611.

Sorrentino, M., Sicilia, M., & Howlett, M. (2018). Understanding co-production as a new public governance tool. Policy and Society, 37(3), 277–293.

Soszyński, D., Sowińska-Świerkosz, B., Stokowski, P. A., & Tucki, A. (2018). Spatial arrangements of tourist villages: Implications for the integration of residents and tourists. Tourism Geographies, 20(5), 770–790.

Steen, M., Manschot, M., & Nicole, D. K. (2011). Benefits of co-design in service design projects. International Journal of Design, 5(2), 53–60.

Steen, T. (2021). Citizens' motivations for co-production: Willingness, ability and opportunity at play. In The Palgrave Handbook of Co-production of Public Services and Outcomes (pp. 507–525). London UK: Palgrave Macmillan. Edited by Elke Loeffler, Tony Bovaird.

Steen, T., Brandsen, T., & Verschuere, B. (2018). The dark side of co-creation and co-production: Seven evils. In Co-production and Co-creation (pp. 284–293). New York, USA: Routledge. Edited By Taco Brandsen, Bram Verschuere, Trui Steen.

Steiner, A., Farmer, J., Yates, S., Moran, M., & Carlisle, K. (2023). How to systematically analyze co-production to inform future policies? Introducing 5Ws of co-production. Public Administration Review, 83(3), 503–521.

Stewart, J., & Clarke, M. (1987). The public service orientation: Issues and dilemmas. Public Administration, 65(2), 161–177.

Stoker, G. (2006). Public value management: A new narrative for networked governance? The American Review of Public Administration, 36(1), 41–57.

Straussman, J. D. (2022). Co-production at the front line: A user reflection on theory and practice. Public Management Review, 24, 1–7.

Strokosch, K., & Osborne, S. (2016). Asylum seekers and the co-production of public services: Understanding the implications for social inclusion and citizenship. Journal of Social Policy, 45(4), 673–690.

Strokosch, K., & Osborne, S. (2020). Co-experience, co-production and co-governance: An ecosystem approach to the analysis of value creation. Policy & Politics, 48(3), 425–442.

Strokosch, K., & Osborne, S. P. (2016). Asylum seekers and the co-production of public services: Understanding the implications for social inclusion and citizenship. Journal of Social Policy, 45(4), 673–690.

Thomsen, M. K. (2017). Citizen co-production: The influence of self-efficacy perception and knowledge of how to co-produce. American Review of Public Administration, 47(3), 340–353.

Thomsen, M. K., & Jakobsen, M. (2015). Influencing citizen coproduction by sending encouragement and advice: A field experiment. International Public Management Journal, 18(2), 286–303.

Tria, G., & Valotti, G. (Eds.). (2012). Reforming the Public Sector: How to Achieve Better Transparency, Service, and Leadership. Washington, DC: Brookings Institution Press.

Trischler, J., & Charles, M. (2019). The application of a service ecosystems lens to public policy analysis and design. Journal of Public Policy & Marketing, 38(1), 19–35.

Trischler, J., & Westman-Trischler, J. (2022). Design for experience – a public service design approach in the age of digitalization. Public Management Review, 24(8), 1251–1270.

Trischler, J., Kristensson, P., & Scott, D. (2018). Team diversity and its management in a co-design team. Journal of Service Management, 29(1), 120–145.

Trischler, J., Pervan, S. J., Kelly, S. J., & Scott, D. (2018). The value of codesign: The effect of customer involvement in service design teams. Journal of Service Research, 21(1), 75–100.

Trischler, J., Dietrich, T., & Rundle-Thiele, S. (2019). Co-design: From expert-to user-driven ideas in public service design. Public Management Review, 21(11), 1595–1619.

Tuurnas, S. (2015). Learning to co-produce: The perspective of public service professionals. International Journal of Public Sector Management, 28(7), 583–598.

Vafeas, M., Hughes, T., & Hilton, T. (2016). Antecedents to value diminution: A dyadic perspective. Marketing Theory, 16(4), 469–491.

Vallance, P., Tewdwr-Jones, M., & Kempton, L. (2020). Building collaborative platforms for urban innovation: Newcastle city futures as a quadruple helix intermediary. European Urban and Regional Studies, 27(4), 325–341.

Van Eijk, C. J. A., & Steen, T. P. S. (2014). Why people co-produce: Analysing citizens' perceptions on co-planning engagement in health care services. Public Management Review, 16(3), 358–382.

Van Tatenhove, J., Edelenbos, J., & Klok, P. J. (2010). Power and interactive policy-making. Public Administration, 88(3), 609–626.

Vargo, S. L., & Lusch, R. F. (2008). Service-dominant logic: Continuing the evolution. Journal of the Academy of Marketing Science, 36(1), 1–10.

Vargo, S. L., & Lusch, R. F. (2016). Institutions and axioms: An extension and update of service-dominant logic. Journal of the Academy of Marketing Science, 44(1), 5–23.

Vargo, S. L., & Lusch, R. F. (Eds.). (2018). The SAGE handbook of service-dominant logic. California, USA: Sage.

Vargo, S., Akaka, M., & Vaughan, C. (2017). Conceptualizing value: A service-ecosystem view. Journal of Creating Value, 3(2), 117–124.

Vigoda, E., & Golembiewski, R. T. (2001). Citizenship behavior and the spirit of new managerialism – a theoretical framework and challenge for governance. American Review of Public Administration, 31(3), 273–295.

Vink, J., Koskela-Huotari, K., Tronvoll, B., Edvardsson, B., & Wetter-Edman, K. (2021). Service ecosystem design: Propositions, process model, and future research agenda. Journal of Service Research, 24(2), 168–186.

Vlachos, S., Karakosta, C., Sideri, V., Antoniadis, K., & Siskos, A. (2021). Improving the impact of odour nuisance in Thessaloniki: A stakeholder engagement approach. Chemical Engineering Transactions, 85, 133–138.

Vohland, K., Land-Zandstra, A., Ceccaroni, L., et al. (2021). The Science of Citizen Science (p. 529). Springer Nature, Switzerland, AG.

Voorberg, W., Tummers, L., Bekkers, V., et al. (2015). Co-creation and citizen involvement in social innovation: A comparative case study across 7 EU-countries. A report from LISPE research project work package, 2.

Voorberg, W., Jilke, S., Tummers, L., & Bekkers, V. (2018). Financial rewards do not stimulate coproduction: Evidence from two experiments. Public Administration Review, 78(6), 864–873.

Voorberg, W. H., Bekkers, V. J., & Tummers, L. G. (2015). A systematic review of co-creation and co-production: Embarking on the social innovation journey. Public Management Review, 17(9), 1333–1357.

Weibel, A., Rost, K., & Osterloh, M. (2010). Pay for performance in the public sector – benefits and (hidden) costs. Journal of Public Administration Research and Theory, 20(2), 387–412.

White, O. (1971). Social change and administrative adaptation. In F. Marini (Ed.), Toward a New Public Administration: The Minnowbrook Perspective (59–83). Scanton: Chandler.

Williams, B. N., Kang, S. C., & Johnson, J. (2016). (Co)-contamination as the dark side of co-production: Public value failures in co-production processes. Public Management Review, 18(5), 692–717.

Williams, I., & Shearer, H. (2011). Appraising public value: Past, present and futures. Public Administration, 89(4), 1367–1384.

Wilson, J. (1973). Introduction to Social Movements. New York: Basic Books.

Yang, K. (2016). Creating public value and institutional innovations across boundaries: An integrative process of participation, legitimation and implementation. Public Administration Review, November/December, 76(6), 873–885.

Cambridge Elements ≡

Public and Nonprofit Administration

Andrew Whitford
University of Georgia
Andrew Whitford is Alexander M. Crenshaw Professor of Public Policy in the School of
Public and International Affairs at the University of Georgia. His research centers on strategy
and innovation in public policy and organization studies.

Robert Christensen
Brigham Young University
Robert Christensen is professor and George Romney Research Fellow in the Marriott
School at Brigham Young University. His research focuses on prosocial and antisocial
behaviors and attitudes in public and nonprofit organizations.

About the Series
The foundation of this series are cutting-edge contributions on emerging topics and
definitive reviews of keystone topics in public and nonprofit administration,
especially those that lack longer treatment in textbook or other formats. Among
keystone topics of interest for scholars and practitioners of public and nonprofit
administration, it covers public management, public budgeting and finance,
nonprofit studies, and the interstitial space between the public and nonprofit sectors,
along with theoretical and methodological contributions, including quantitative,
qualitative and mixed-methods pieces.

The Public Management Research Association
The Public Management Research Association improves public governance by advancing
research on public organizations, strengthening links among interdisciplinary scholars, and
furthering professional and academic opportunities in public management.

Cambridge Elements ᵉ

Public and Nonprofit Administration

Elements in the Series

A full series listing is available at: www.cambridge.org/EPNP

Printed in the United States
by Baker & Taylor Publisher Services